CALLED TO PREACH

The Warrack Lectures
1968–69

CALLED
TO PREACH

Stuart W. McWilliam

THE SAINT ANDREW PRESS
EDINBURGH

Published by
The Saint Andrew Press
121 George Street, Edinburgh.

SBN 7152 0046 1

Printed in Great Britain
by Econoprint Ltd., Edinburgh
and bound by Henderson and Bissett,
Edinburgh.

CONTENTS

To the congregations of
Sherwood Church, Paisley,
Beechgrove Church, Aberdeen
and
Wellington Church, Glasgow,
with affection and gratitude

PREFACE

Any Warrack Lecturer today is confronted by two major problems: first, the ghosts of his distinguished predecessors many of them, happily, very substantial ghosts, who must surely have said all that there is to say on the subject of Preaching: second, the awareness that there is, at this time, a widespread suspicion of preaching, a questioning of its value, a loss of confidence in its power. Concerning the first of these problems, I would simply remind the reader that these lectures were founded for the benefit of students preparing for the ministry of the Church. Each lecturer, therefore, faces a new generation of students to whom the same kind of things need to be said and I have tried to say them in the idiom of today and against the background of the world of today. As to the second problem, its existence provides the principal reason for my acceptance of this task. I am convinced that nothing is more necessary for the Church today than a renewal of concern about preaching. Looking back through the whole course of Christian history I cannot discover any great movement of religion which was not rooted and grounded in preaching. Whether it be the remarkably rapid expansion of the Early Church, the Franciscan Movement, the Reformation, the Wesleyan Revival or the great Missionary Out-thrust of the nineteenth century, preaching has been central to them all. Any search for a new pattern of mission, any attempt to devise a new shape for the life of the Church, which fails to accord to preaching its central place is bound to be inadequate. It is out of this conviction that these lectures were written.

In preparing the lectures for publication I have not attempted to disguise the fact that they are lectures and have tried to retain the directness which belongs naturally to them. This seemed to me preferable to attempting to give them a more polished literary form which would have altered their original character.

I have to thank the Trustees of the Warrack Lectures who honoured me by inviting me to deliver them and the staff and students of Christ's College, Aberdeen, New College, Edinburgh, St. Mary's College, St. Andrews, and Trinity College, Glasgow, for their courtesy and the generous welcome they gave to the lectures when they were delivered. My thanks are also due to the Rev. Alastair Dingwall who revised the proofs.

If these lectures prove to be of assistance not only to others who are engaged in the demanding task of preaching but also to some of those who Sunday by Sunday are involved with the preacher in the proclamation of the gospel and if, above all, they help to emphasise the primary importance of preaching today I shall be amply rewarded.

Stuart W. McWilliam

Wellington Church,
Glasgow.

I

THE PREACHER'S TASK

'Every one who calls upon the name of the Lord will be saved.' But how are men to call upon him in whom they have not believed? And how are they to believe in him of whom they have never heard? And how are they to hear without a preacher? And how can men preach unless they are sent? As it is written, 'How beautiful are the feet of those who preach good news!' But they have not all heeded the Gospel; for Isaiah says, 'Lord, who has believed what he has heard from us?' So faith comes from what is heard, and what is heard comes by the preaching of Christ. [1]

Much of what I have to say in the lectures which follow will be in the nature of an expansion and elaboration of these verses. This, for me, is what preaching is about! This is why I am a minister. I believe that 'every one who calls upon the name of the Lord will be saved'. I believe that men cannot hear without a preacher. I believe that men cannot preach 'unless they are sent', unless they feel compulsion laid upon them to preach — 'Woe to me if I preach not the Gospel'. Not 'Woe to the world if I do not preach the Gospel' but 'Woe to me if I do not preach the Gospel'. I believe that 'faith comes from what is heard' and 'what is heard comes by the preaching of Christ'.

Today concern is frequently expressed about the grave shortage of candidates for the ordained ministry of the Church. This situation is not peculiar to the Church of Scotland: it is to be found in all denominations. Nor is it confined to the churches in Britain: it is to be found also among the churches in Europe and America. Indeed, in these latter the problem

1 Romans 10 : 13–17 (R.S.V.)

1

is further complicated by the fact that a considerable proportion of those who undergo training for the ministry elect thereafter to take up what are called 'extra-parochial' appointments. This is particularly true in Germany and in the United States but I suspect that it is a phenomenon which is likely to become increasingly apparent in every church.

There are probably a variety of reasons for this and, no doubt, some of these will be revealed by the various committees and commissions which have been set up to examine recruitment for the ministry. I am convinced that a principal reason is a lack of conviction about the importance of preaching.

We frequently hear it said that the day of the preaching ministry is over; and there are even those who make this observation with what appears to be a considerable measure of satisfaction; as though the decay of the preaching ministry were 'a consummation devoutly to be wished'. This is an attitude which I find difficult to understand and impossible to accept.

In the Reformed tradition the preaching ministry has always had a central place. But the centrality of preaching surely goes much farther back than the Reformation; it is rooted in the New Testament. When Jesus came forth on his mission to men, he came preaching. When he sent out his disciples, he sent them out to preach. Whatever other things they were to do, this was their primary task 'to preach the Gospel'. This, let there be no dubiety about it, is our first task: to preach the good news of God. It is to this task that we are called. It is for this task that we are prepared. There is no escape from the demand laid upon us to be God's heralds, to declare what he has done, to rehearse his mighty act in Jesus Christ for the salvation of men.

This, as I see it, is the chief function of the minister, to be a preacher. It is not one of the possible or alternative roles for the minister but the first demand upon him.

There are many ways in which a man may serve the Gospel and advance the cause of the Kingdom of God. Preachers are not the only ones who can be witnesses to the power of the Gospel. The Ministry of the Church to the World is, and must always be, the Ministry of the whole Church, of the whole people of God, and in this Ministry every Christian man and woman has a part and share. But within this Ministry is the ministry to which we are called, the 'ministry of the Word and Sacrament', and at the heart of this lies the call to preach.

Sometimes the pastoral office of the minister may be set over and against his preaching as if it were a possible and acceptable alternative and it may be said of a man: 'He is a good pastor but no preacher'. But to be a pastor is not an alternative to being a preacher. The pastoral office can be, should be, and is being exercised by many in the Church who are not ministers; and all of us, who have been in the parish ministry for any length of time, would be prepared to concede that it is sometimes exercised more effectively by them than by us, that there are elders and members who have gifts for personal work which far surpass our own.

For the minister however it is an integral part of his pastoral office to preach. For him, to be a good pastor, he must be a preacher. I am not speaking now about oratorical gifts or pulpit styles or beautiful resonant voices; these are flim-flam. I am saying that it is an inescapable part of our pastoral care of people to preach. We cannot plead, in extenuation of our failures in preaching, that there are so many other good and useful and helpful things we do, any more than a doctor could argue, as his justification for being a doctor, that while he did not know much about medicine, he could help people in other ways. We are called to preach. We are ordained to the ministry of the Word and Sacrament, but to separate the ministry of the Sacrament from that of the Word and to suggest that the reason for our existence is to be found in the authority given to us to administer the sacraments of the Church is to take a perilously priestly view of the ministry and one which would not be in accord with the traditions of the Reformed Churches.

In what is still one of the finest books on preaching, P.T. Forsyth writes:

> The one great preacher in history I would contend is the Church. And the first business of the individual preacher is to enable the Church to preach. Yet so that he is not its echo but its living voice, not the echo of its consciousness but the organ of its Gospel. He is to preach to the Church from the Gospel so that with the Church he may preach the Gospel to the world. He is so to preach to the Church that he shall also preach from the Church. That is to say, he must be a sacrament to the Church that with the Church he may become a missionary to the world. [1]

This is indeed a very high view of the preacher's task, but it is not too high! If we minimise the importance of preaching, the inevitable result will be an increasing confusion and uncertainty about the role of the minister, and an increasing unwillingness on the part of men to see this as their Christian vocation. What is this man for, if it is not to preach? What is he supposed to do or be, if he is not to be a preacher? The minister does not belong to a special priestly caste within the

1 *Positive Preaching and the Modern Mind*, P.T. Forsyth,
Independent Press, London, 1964, p 53.

Church but, within the ministry of the whole Church, he is a man who feels himself called to serve in this particular way, to this particular task of preaching; whose call has been tested, in so far as the Church can test it, and confirmed by the Church which has then authorised him to exercise this ministry.

The Essential Nature of the Preacher's Task.

He is to declare, proclaim, tell forth what God has done and is doing in Jesus Christ. The message which he declares is given. It is not something which he dreams up for himself. It is not created *ex-nihilo* by him. It is not the product of his own wisdom. It does not depend upon the fertility of his imagination. The central message of the faith is given. It is rooted in history, in what God has done, and the pulpit exists for the proclamation of this. As P.T. Forsyth has written:

> A man is not invited into the pulpit to say how things strike him from his angle, any more than he is expected to lay bare to the public the private recesses of his soul . . . . He is not in the pulpit primarily as the place where he can get most scope for his own individuality and most freedom for his own idiosyncrasies. He is there as the servant both of the Word and of the Church to do a certain work, to declare a certain message, to discharge a certain trust, He is not in the pulpit as the roomiest place he has found to enable him to be himself and develop his genius.... There is put into the preacher's hands a trust, a message which is not merely like the artist's — the subjective trust of genius with a responsibility as to how it shall be used; but is the objective trust of the Gospel, of a positive word which he must deliver, however it may affect his self-culture. Any genius he has can but enrich his Gospel.' [1]

1 Ibid. pp. 70–71

The message then is given! It has been revealed. The task of the preacher is to declare it.

At first sight, this might seem to reduce the role of the preacher to that of a news-caster who, in a studiously impersonal manner, carefully avoiding any inflexions or emphases lest they reveal a personal bias, involvement or interpretation, declares; 'This is the news!' This would be a caricature of what is meant by preaching. The Word which the preacher declares is contained in the scriptures of the Old and New Testaments. It is revealed but it is also hidden. It has to be interpreted. It has to be made plain. Therefore true preaching must always be Biblical Preaching. The Bible is the preacher to the preacher. The Word of God is to be found there. The preacher is to proclaim what God has done, and is doing, through the exposition of the scriptures.

This does not mean that, having found a topic upon which we wish to preach, we search the scriptures desperately to find some text upon which we can hang our discourse — a practice which nearly always leads to a misuse of the Bible. Nor does it mean that we use the Bible as a collection of proof texts to support our own theological presuppositions — even if these happen to be true. Much of what passes for Biblical preaching in certain circles falls into this category. It is the preaching of ideas which may, or may not, be Biblical in their origin, larded by innumerable quotations from scripture, usually wrenched out of their context but always prefaced by the formula 'the Bible says...' Doubtless, in many such instances, the preacher would be horrified were you to accuse him of not being Biblical. For it is his proud boast that he is always Biblical — and he would perhaps point out that much of his sermon was composed of direct quotations from the Bible.

Nevertheless this is not Biblical preaching. This is not preaching from the Bible. This is using the Bible as the servant rather than being the servant of the Bible.

Biblical preaching is preaching which allows the Bible to speak, to be heard. It necessarily involves an honest study of the passage to discover what the writer actually said, the circumstances in which it was said and what it meant to those to whom it was first said. But it does not stop there. We must discover what this means for us today in the light of God's revelation in Jesus Christ and in the context of the people to whom we speak. Obviously the preacher must study the Bible but if he is to be an interpreter, he must also know the language of the people to whom he speaks and must be able to translate the truth in terms which they can understand. This is much more than simply a matter of words and syntax, important though these may be. The preacher must know the men and women to whom he speaks and the world in which they live. I believe that it was Dr. George Macleod who used to tell the story of a minister who had preached a series of sermons on the topic "Questions men are asking". When he reached the end of his series he asked one of the young men in the congregation what he had thought of it and received the reply: "It was very interesting; the only thing is that no one is asking these questions."

The simple Gospel is anything but simple when we have to try to make plain its implications amid the bewildering complexities of the modern world to men and women who are caught up in these complexities. The preacher has a dual responsibility; to the Word and to the people to whom he must declare that Word. This is what makes preaching so demanding and frightening a task. It is not simply a mechanical recitation of certain facts but involves the interpretation and translation of the meaning of these facts in terms which will be intelligible and meaningful for those who listen. It requires the discipline of prayer and study — study both of the Bible and of the world to which the message of the Bible is to be preached. It is frightening because where interpretation is involved there is always the danger of a man confusing God's Word with his own word and while 'the foolishness of God is wiser than men', our foolishness is something very different! Thus no man should approach the task of preaching without a measure of holy fear.

"The Word of God is a red hot iron", says the Curé de Torcy in George Bernanos's moving novel *The Diary of a Country Priest*. "And you, who preach it, 'ud go picking it up with a pair of tongs for fear of burning yourself; you don't dare get hold of it with both hands! It's too funny! Why the priest who descends from the pulpit of Truth with a mouth like a hen's vent, a little hot but pleased with himself; he's not been preaching. At best he's been purring like a tabby cat." And later he cries: "The Word of God! Give me back my Word, the judge will say on the last day. When you think about what certain people will have to unpack on that occasion it's no laughing matter I assure you."[1] Nevertheless it 'pleased God by the foolishness of preaching to save them that believe.'

1 *The Diary of A Country Priest,* George Bernanos, Fontana Books, London, 1956, pp. 49—54.

THE PREACHER'S TASK

What do we Expect to Happen as the Result of our Preaching?

Do we expect anything to happen? In his *Word of God and The Word of Man* Karl Barth has written:

'On Sunday mornings when the bell rings to call the congregation and the minister to church there is in the air an expectancy that something great, crucial and even momentous is to happen. Above all, here is a man upon whom the expectation of the apparently imminent event seems to rest in a special way. He will enter the pulpit — and here is daring — preach!' [1]

Preachers may perhaps feel that, as far as the average congregation is concerned, this is a somewhat idealised picture of the frame of mind in which they approach worship on Sunday; and we might be inclined to question whether the expectancy which Barth so vividly describes is present — at any rate to the degree which he suggests — but I have no doubt that we would be in agreement that, though the picture may be a somewhat highly coloured one, it represents what ought to be the situation. Sunday after Sunday — twice on most Sundays — we enter the pulpit and dare to preach and, though we may not assume that high level of expectancy upon the part of the congregation which Barth depicts as normal, yet I would insist that there is always a measure of expectancy present; and the man who has ceased to be aware of this had better look to the state of his own soul for he has grown strangely insensitive. Few people come to church today out of mere habit and conventional church-goers have become a rapidly declining minority.

Many years ago I heard the late Dr. Gunn describe

1 Quoted by Leonard Griffith in *God and His People*
Lutterworth Press, London, 1960, p 29.

9

how, during the second world war, Winston Churchill visited Edinburgh and stayed with friends of Dr. Gunn. On Sunday evening Dr. Gunn was invited out to meet the great man who engaged him in conversation. I cannot reproduce the exact words, but it ran something like this:

> 'Dr. Gunn, how many people attend your morning service?'

> 'I suppose around five to six hundred.'

> 'I see! Then you have evensong — an evening service?'

> 'Yes!'

> 'How many people will attend that?'

> 'Oh, not so many, perhaps two hundred.'

> 'Do some of the people who attend your morning service also come to the evening service?'

> 'Yes — perhaps half of those present at the evening service have already been at church in the morning.'

> 'So perhaps six hundred people listen to you every Sunday?'

> 'Yes. I think that would be approximately correct.'

Then Churchill said; 'If I were to speak twice a Sunday in the same place to the same people on my own subject, politics, at the end of six months there would be no one there to listen to me.'

Sunday after Sunday there are people there in church, perhaps with mixed motives and for a variety of reasons, but always among them there are those who have come to hear if there is 'any word from the Lord' — a word from beyond which will meet their need. Moreover the preacher should be aware that, just as no man ever enters the same river twice, so no preacher, however long he has been in a charge, ever speaks twice to exactly the same congregation. The names may be

10

the same. the faces may be the same, but since last he addressed them, things have happened to men and women in that congregation which have changed them; big things, little things, good things, bad things. The man who only last week sat there and wondered whether the service would be over in time for him to get home, have lunch, change and be on the first tee by two-thirty may, because of what has happened to him in the interval, be listening, almost with desperation, for some word from the Lord, hoping to catch something which will speak to his situation. The woman who, only last Sunday, was living in what seemed to be a secure and sheltered world, may this Sunday be facing a personal crisis which threatens to disrupt and destroy that world. Every week there are events, encounters, experiences, which, subtly or violently, affect the lives of some men and women in the congregation before you and make them *more* or *less* eager to hear the Word of God. Whatever the level of expectancy in the congregation it should always be high in the preacher. God help him if ever he reaches that sorry state where preaching becomes just another chore to be tackled; where a man enters the pulpit without any sense of anticipation, any quickening of the pulse, without the conviction that he is sharing in God's deed, God's action. To return to our question; 'What do we expect to happen?' Carlyle wrote of the pulpit:

'That a man should stand there and speak of spiritual things to me is beautiful even in its obscurity and decadence, it is among the beautifullest and most touching objects one sees on the earth. This speaking man has indeed, in these times, wandered terribly far from the point; has, alas, as it were, totally lost sight of the point, yet at bottom what have we to compare with him? Of all such functionaries boarded and lodged on the industry of modern Europe is there one

on earth worthier or the board he has? The speaking
function, with all our writing and printing functions
has a perennial place, could he but find the point
again.' [1]

What is the point? We have defined preaching in terms
of the declaration of the mighty acts of God through
the exposition of the Bible. But what is the aim of this?
It is not primarily to instruct, to give information. There
is, as C.H. Dodd has pointed out, a distinction between
Kerygma and *Didache,* between preaching and teaching.
There will be teaching in preaching but this is not the
first purpose of preaching. A sermon is not a lecture and
the pulpit is not really the place for teaching, anymore
than the classroom is the place for preaching.

This indeed is one of the major problems with
which we are confronted to-day that there is a very
great need for teaching in the Church but most of us are
still searching for the right place and the right time to
do this. Teaching demands a quite different setting from
preaching. In teaching there must be an opportunity for
question and answer, for people to interrupt and
demand information, for them to be able to say, 'Stop!
I do not understand you! Make yourself more plain!'
There must be room for discussion and debate. It is one
of the functions of the minister to teach: but in my
view this is not the primary aim of preaching. It may be
that this is the kind of use to which our second service
should be put — that it ought to be devoted specifically
to a teaching session. But one would have to recognise
that, in this event, it cannot simply be a curtailed form
of the morning service. The whole nature of it will
require to be radically changed and perhaps, also, the
place in which it is held, since even the physical

1 Quoted by Samuel Miller in *But Find The Point Again,*
Union Seminary Quarterly Review, March 1960.

construction of our places of worship is a hindrance to teaching, apart from the fact that the purpose to which they are normally devoted would, rightly or wrongly, tend to have a somewhat repressive and inhibiting effect upon the free and lively interchange of ideas which would be considered a prerequisite in a teaching situation. I am very conscious that ministers of my generation were not trained in teaching methods. This is a defect which I understand is being remedied to-day.

Preaching is not, in the first instance, teaching. Faith is not the giving of assent to a series of propositions, but commitment in a personal relationship with God. A colleague has told me of a man whom he used to visit regularly and with whom he had long theological discussions. This man, he claimed, was quite exceptionally well-read in theology. Mention any of the great theological works, he had read it! But the conversations took place in a cell in Peterhead prison where the man was serving a long sentence — and not his first — for his crimes against society! It is possible to know all the theological answers and still to be very far from the Kingdom of God. It is possible to be very inarticulate, even theologically illiterate, and still to know Jesus as Lord. Preaching is concerned with Faith.

The success or failure of a preacher does not rest upon the ability of men and women to pass an examination paper on what he said last Sunday. There was a time when I thought it important that people should remember my sermons, and I was frequently disturbed to discover how little they did remember. I now realise that I cannot, without considerable effort, recall what my sermon was on Sunday morning two or three weeks ago and, therefore, it is hardly reasonable to expect that others should. It probably took me anything from eight to ten hours to prepare that sermon. I was completely immersed in it before I entered the pulpit. If I cannot now recall it, how should I expect those who heard it only once to remember it? Fortunately this does not matter, since the primary aim of the preacher is not to give instruction. It is rather that men and women should meet with God and make their response to Him. It is for this that the preacher prays. If I did not believe that, somehow, through my words the Word of God will come to some men and women in the congregation and evoke a response from them; that somehow through my words they will hear the Word of God to them in their situation, whatever that situation may be: if I did not believe this I would give up preaching immediately. But this is at once the miracle, the mystery and the glory of preaching that this does happen, that through it men and women do hear the Word of God and make their response to it.

It is a not uncommon experience for a minister to have someone say to him: 'I still remember a sermon you preached five years ago in which you said .....' and here follows what purports to be a verbatim quotation. 'It made a tremendous difference to me at that particular time in my life and I have never forgotten it!' He had never forgotten it! But the preacher may well have forgotten that he said it. Indeed he may even feel almost convinced that he did not say it and wish that he had. This is of no importance. The important thing is that this is what that person heard, that this was, for them, at that particular time in their experience, the Word of God which spoke to their condition. What they are really remembering is not a sermon but a response which they made to a truth which that day laid hold upon them. At such times a man realises what it means to speak of the preacher as being 'a sacrament to the Church', a means of grace as important as the elements but no more important. And, for your comfort, may I add that I believe this is something which happens continually when the Word of God is faithfully preached though you may only occasionally be given evidence of its happening.

Who shall Preach?

The Church, in so far as it is able to do so, tests a man's vocation and then, being satisfied, rightly insists that he shall undergo the discipline of academic study to enable him to exercise his vocation in the ministry of the Word and Sacrament. But how shall men preach unless they are sent? I would not dare to attempt to analyse the nature of any man's call to the ministry. As I have indicated, my understanding of the ministry sees it as belonging within the ministry of the whole people of God. Nevertheless I am convinced that no man has the right to preach unless he believes that what he has to tell is the most important tidings ever announced to the world, and is persuaded that nothing matters so much as that this Gospel should be made known.

Today we have an extraordinary situation in which an increasing awareness of mission, as the reason for the Church's existence, is often accompanied by an increasing suspicion of proselytising. Indeed this has become almost a dirty word with associations of intolerance, arrogance and aggressiveness. If what is being condemned is the attempt to thrust upon others my set of theological formulae, my form of worship, my cultural patterns, then I too would condemn this. But I have the feeling that something more is being called in question, namely the legitimacy of the desire that men should know what God has done for them in Christ and should respond to it.

15

What is the purpose of the mission of the Church if it is not this? What is the aim of preaching if it is not this? Who shall preach? The man who believes that the Good News he has to declare is of supreme importance. No man should preach unless he cares so much for people that he considers it as important that men should hear as that God has spoken. The passion for the message and the passion for men are twin passions. Thus Paul could say, 'For to me to live is Christ' and also, 'I could wish that myself were accursed from Christ for my brethren.'

II

THE PREACHER'S WORLD

The religious climate in Britain in the second half of the Twentieth Century has been described as follows:

> 'The issue today is not whether this or that Christian doctrine or formulation is satisfactory but whether the Christian system is credible at all. It is not profitable to dispute whether the Virgin Mary should be called the Mother of God, when men are in doubt about the existence of God himself.' [1]

While we in the churches may be arguing about what is meant by 'apostolic succession' and whether the acceptance of some form of episcopacy is a prerequisite if there is to be a union of the churches; and what is meant by the 'real presence' in the Communion; and whether there is any valid theological barrier to the ordination of women to the ministry; the world outside, the world for which the Church exists, is not in the least interested in what it would dismiss as our theological minutiae. What is being called in question there, is whether there is a God at all and, if there is, can it be truly said that he has revealed himself in Jesus Christ; and, if he did, what does this mean? What is being questioned are the central, fundamental claims of the Christian Faith and to those who are questioning these much of our theological debate seems utterly irrelevant, even where it is comprehensible! This is the age of the scientist who has, literally, searched the heavens and found no evidence of God; the age of the surgeon who has explored the human body and found no separate entity which could be identified as the soul of man; the

---

1 *My Cherry Tree*, Nathaniel Micklem, London, 1966, p 31.

age of the psychologist who has taught us to distrust convictions of any kind and to distrust them the more, the more passionately they are held, as being all too easily the product of our own desires, the dogmatising of our own wishes. This is the age in which we have to preach, an age in which, not surprisingly, the pulpit is suspect for many reasons, some of which we shall now proceed to examine more closely.

A Scientific and Technological Age.

This is an age in which, because of its splendid achievements, science enjoys enormous prestige. For the great mass of ordinary people today science represents reason, truth, that which can be clearly verified. I am concerned here, not with how scientists think of science, but with the beliefs which the laymen, the non-scientists, entertain concerning it. They are likely to be much more arrogant in their claims regarding science than the scientists themselves, who often seem to be very humble — more humble indeed than many theologians!

For a very large number of people the most damning criticism which can be made of any theory or argument is that it is unscientific, and they believe that this is a criticism which can justifiably be levelled against the Bible. To them it appears that science has made belief in the Bible and in the God of the Bible untenable. Christians appear to them to alternate between an obscurantist dogmatism which steadfastly refuses to accept the findings of modern science and a feeble apologetic witness to the truth of the Bible, which is designed to offend no one and which arouses nothing but contempt in those who feel that, in all seriousness, they must challenge this truth. Preachers may argue that they find no difficulty in reconciling their faith with the discoveries of a scientific age, their belief in the authority of scripture with an acceptance of the authority of science in its own realm. But I suspect that many, even within the Church, among our contemporaries are convinced that they can achieve this reconciliation only at the expense of some kind of double think on their part. I am further persuaded that this state of affairs is largely our own fault: I mean the fault of the preachers. The majority of people do not know where we stand in our attitude to the Bible.

They suspect that we are literalists when it suits us, and liberals when it does not. Despite all our theological training and our Old and New Testament studies, very little of how we believe the Bible is to be read and used and understood and what we mean by the authority of scripture has got through to our congregations, and still less to the world outside. Whether this is because we are afraid of disturbing the faith of the simple, which is just another way of saying that we are afraid of trusting our congregations, or because we are too lazy to make the effort, or because we assume that what is commonplace to us must be commonplace to them and to everyone else, I leave you to decide. In a scientific age, there is a paramount need to make plain to men where we stand in relation to the Bible.

A scientific age tends to be an age of literalism, one which finds the language of religion, which is more akin to the language of poetry than that of science, difficult. As an army chaplain I used to conduct Padre's Hours and I recall a young soldier who challenged me on the story of Noah and the Ark. 'Do you expect us to believe,' said he, 'that while it took thousands of men several years to build the Queen Mary (then the biggest liner in the world) Noah and his sons could, in a comparatively short time, build a boat big enough to take at least two of every kind of bird, beast, reptile and insect in the world? And', he added for good measure, 'they would have had to cut their own timber too.' I said that I did not expect him to believe this, and then I tried to explain to him the truth contained within the story of the Flood; a truth which, though not necessarily an accurate scientific account of what happened, is nevertheless true. I suspect he thought that I was indulging in some kind of double talk, because for him the issue seemed so plain and straightforward. Either the story was literally true or it was not true at all!

His attitude is characteristic of a very large number of people in an age which needs to be helped to understand again the language of religion: to see that it is not the same as the language of science. They have to have it made plain to them what the Bible is about. It is about God in his dealing with men. Because the Biblical writers were ignorant of the theories of evolution, nuclear physics, modern cosmology, it is automatically assumed by many that this discredits what they have to say about God. They were not propounding scientific theories. They were talking about God; and what they have to say about God is as relevant to men living in the twentieth century space age as it was to men who believed that the earth was flat and shaped like a saucer. Much has been made in recent years of the fact that the men of the Bible thought they were living in a three tiered universe with heaven above, hell below and earth in the middle. Perhaps they did! But what does this have to do with faith in God? If one discredits their message because of their primitive cosmology, it is akin to claiming that Shakespeare's penetrating analyses of human nature can be discounted because he knew less chemistry than any thirteen year old child does today.

The primitive cosmology of the Bible is utterly irrelevant, and that people do not see that it is utterly irrelevant is a most damaging criticism of our preaching and teaching.

Personally, I question whether the Biblical writers were nearly as naive as many of their modern critics naively assume they were, when they accuse them of believing in a 'God up there'; of 'localising God .

'If I ascend up into heaven, thou art there:
if I make my bed in hell, behold, thou art there.
If I take the wings of the morning, and dwell in
the uttermost parts of the sea; even there. . . '

Surely it is evident that for the man who wrote this, God was everywhere and it was impossible to escape from His presence. I doubt whether the men of the Bible would have been dismayed or discouraged by the report of the Russian astronaut that he found no evidence of the presence of God in his orbit through space. They would probably have said that if he rejected the God of Abraham, of Isaac and of Jacob, the God who revealed Himself in history, he would hardly be likely to find God in the solar system. For the Bible is concerned with a God who reveals Himself in history rather than through the natural world. It is important that in our preaching today we should make this plain. The concern of the scientist with the natural world can neither prove nor disprove the existence of God. In our preaching we must help men and women to understand the language of the Bible and to distinguish it from the language of science. This means that we must beware of using the Bible as if it were a scientific textbook. We know that in the past men have done this; and we know of the bitter and destructive conflicts precipitated by this misuse of the Bible, conflicts over cosmology, evolution, anaesthetics and a host of other subjects. We may not be aware of the temptation to indulge in this kind of exercise today, yet it is present. All those misguided attempts to prove that this or that Biblical writer was anticipating the latest scientific discovery are to be deplored; not only because they are not particularly subtle attempts to assert the authority of the Bible in a realm in which it makes no claim to be authoritative, but also because they teach people to read the Bible in the wrong way, to look for the wrong things from it. All those ingenious attempts to harmonise some Biblical text with the latest piece of scientific or medical information culled from *The Reader's Digest* can do great damage by implicitly suggesting that this was the purpose of the Biblical writer, and thereby deflecting attention from his true purpose of speaking about God in His dealings with men. Typical of this clever but dangerous practice would be the use of the text from Ezekiel, "A new heart also will I give you," as providing a justification for heart transplantation.

A further problem which arises for preaching in a scientific age is to be found in the differing conceptions of truth which prevail in such an age. There is a tendency for truth to be equated with scientific facts, and for men to fall into the error of imagining that 'the Truth' is something which can be reached by the simple if laborious process of adding all the facts together, as brick is added to brick in the erection of a building. Thus, the argument would run, if we assemble all the facts about the natural world, how it works, the rules which govern it, then the sum total of these facts will constitute the truth about the natural world. Similarly if we can add up all the facts about man, biological, chemical, bio-chemical, physiological, psychological, we shall be able to reach the truth about man. Yet if truth is to be understood in this way as the sum total of the facts, then it becomes increasingly evident that it is impossible for any man ever to know it, since in science alone the volume of facts is so great that no human being could ever grasp them all. It is no exaggeration to say that the experts in one field of science are themselves quite incapable of understanding what the experts in another field are doing. They know more and more about less and less, and less and less about more and more. There is a story, with a fine touch of irony, which tells how men linked up all the electronic brains and computers in the world together and then fed into this gigantic master brain every single fact discovered by human wisdom. Having done this, they then asked the million dollar question: 'Is there a God?' and back came the answer: 'There is now!' This is how modern man builds his tower of Babel, laying fact upon fact in the belief that thus he can reach ultimate truth; and the significant thing is that it leads to a confusion of tongues, so that men in one field of knowledge can no longer even understand what those in another field are talking about.

The truth we handle and declare is not the sum total of the facts but the reality which lies behind the facts, that in which, or rather he in whom all things cohere. This is what we dare to preach and can, without fear, continue to preach in a scientific age.

The Old Authorities Questioned.

In an age of questioning it is inevitable that the pulpit should be suspect. That any man should declare: "Thus saith the Lord" is bound to be called in question. There are two dangers against which we need constantly to be on our guard. The first, that in reaction, a reaction largely motivated by fear, we claim to know more than in fact we do know. And the second, also motivated by fear, that we suffer a loss of nerve and claim to know less than we have a right and duty to do. In this context I would remind you of these familiar words of St. Paul from the thirteenth chapter of the first letter to the Corinthians where he says: 'We know in part....' For all his radiant certainty concerning that which God had done for him and for all men in Jesus Christ, for all his unshakeable conviction of the triumphant adequacy of Christ, Paul did not claim to know all the answers, to have solved all the mysteries. He admitted that his knowledge was partial, his understanding limited, his vision incomplete. 'Now we see through a glass darkly' or 'Now we see baffling reflections in a mirror'.

It is essential that we should be prepared to admit that "we know in part", that we should be prepared to admit this not only to ourselves but to others; and not only to those others who share our faith and from whom, therefore, we may expect to receive sympathy and understanding, but also to those who do not share our faith and who may indeed seem determined to destroy it. When hard pressed in an argument there is always a danger of holding stubbornly to a position which, in our heart of hearts, we realise is indefensible, because to surrender it might be interpreted by an opponent as a sign of weakness. When this temptation arises, as sometimes it does in the course of our attempts to defend the faith, we must resist it; recognising that it is of the devil. God cannot be defended by dishonesty; neither can he be defeated by the truth, from whatever source that truth appears to come. All too often in the past the preacher has appeared, in the eyes of the world, as a man claiming to know all the answers and all too often he has given the impression that there was nothing, but nothing, upon

24

which he was not prepared to make a dogmatic pronouncement. He has tried to tell the scientists how they should interpret their discoveries. He has tried to command the artists what they should see. He has tried to instruct the politicians in the details of how they should handle the complex problems with which they are faced.

It may be that something of this authoritarian attitude still remains and I confess that at times I shudder when I hear ecclesiastical dignitaries who appear to be ready, at the drop of a hat, to pontificate on any subject under the sun with the bland assurance of those who know that they are always right. It would, I believe, be a more honest, and certainly a more healing thing, if perhaps more often the world were to hear us confess that we do not know all; we know only in part! We must be prepared to admit the partiality of our knowledge especially when men and women come to us with some of the deep questions of the faith. In their agony and their distress they may often ask questions which we cannot answer. Our desire to help them, and our desire to demonstrate the reasonableness of the faith and therefore, of course, our reasonableness who hold the faith, can all too easily trap us into giving the slick, shallow, superficial answer. *We know only in part.*

But *to know in part is, nevertheless, to know.* It is not to be left in total ignorance, and we must not be so overwhelmed by the burden of what we do not know that we abdicate from our responsibility to proclaim with confidence what we do know. We know that 'God so loved the world that he gave his only begotten Son that whosoever believeth in him should not perish but have everlasting life'. We may not be able to set forth a completely satisfying philosophical answer to the problem of the existence of evil in the world, but we know what, in the last resort, is supremely important, that Christ died for the sin of the world and that, through faith in him, forgiveness of sin and the power to overcome evil are indisputable realities. We may not have any final answer to the problem of suffering but we do know, through Christ, that God is not indifferent to the suffering of men and has entered into it to redeem it from what is its greatest burden, its apparent senselessness. We may not be able to provide a picture of the furnishings of heaven, or a description of the social life of the blessed departed, and we would be ill advised to speculate upon these matters: but we do know that because Christ lives we shall live also. We do not know how, or when, or where the final victory of the Kingdom of God will be fully manifested in the world; but we know that it will come and that all things will be seen to be placed in subjection to Christ, that we are living in the interim period between D Day and V Day. And when men ask: 'What must I do to be saved?' it is carrying non-directive counselling too far to say in reply: 'Well, what do you think yourself?' We know the answer: 'Believe in the Lord Jesus Christ and thou shalt be saved.' I am no advocate for 'The Power of Positive Thinking' but I am increasingly impatient of what might be called the practice of negative preaching, the kind of preaching which appears to be dedicated to the purpose of declaring what the preacher does not believe.

It may sometimes be necessary to remove misconceptions about Christian belief; but what people really want to know and what they have the right to know is what you do believe. It may be that our certainty about what God has done has always to be accompanied by a lack of certainty regarding the finality of some of our formulations and interpretations, but to begin with the latter and never to reach the former is to be neither honest nor responsible.

An Age of Moral Ambiguity.

This, as we are continually being reminded, is a permissive society and therefore anyone who purports to give ethical instruction is immediately suspect. Clearly this presents a very real problem for the preacher since religion must not be divorced from morality. He cannot claim that to have faith is to act, that faith is not simply the giving of assent to a series of propositions but a quality of life and, at the same time, insist that this has nothing to do with morality. It is the responsibility of the preacher to preach the Law, not as over and against the Gospel but with the Gospel.

'How is it possible to proclaim the Gospel without also hearing the Law which says 'Thou shalt love God',' writes Karl Barth. 'To separate the Gospel from the Law in preaching is not Christian.' [1]

Yet it would appear that this is a real danger today. There are those who keep reminding us that to be a Christian is to live under the Gospel and therefore the only law binding upon us is 'the Law of Love'. This sounds all right until you begin to ask 'What is Love? What does Love mean?'

Is Law to be regarded as the contradiction of Love? May it not be the expression of Love? The tendency to regard Law as the denial of Love and freedom from the Law as desirable because it gives freedom to Love is evidence of very shallow superficial thinking against which we must be on our guard. The Law of God was given not in anger but in Love, not in order that man's life might be restricted but in order that it might be liberated, not to stifle life but to allow it to grow and expand.

1 *Prayer and Preaching,* Karl Barth, S.C.M. Press, London, 1964, p 71.

This surely is how the writer of the 19th Psalm regarded the Law:

> 'The law of the Lord is perfect, converting the soul: the testimony of the Lord is sure, making wise the simple. The statutes of the Lord are right, rejoicing the heart: the commandment of the Lord is pure, enlightening the eyes. The fear of the Lord is clean, enduring for ever: the judgments of the Lord are true and righteous altogether. More to be desired are they than gold, yea, than much fine gold: sweeter also than honey and the honeycomb. Moreover by them is thy servant warned: and in keeping of them there is great reward.'

It is a caricature of the Christian Gospel to suggest that Jesus released men from subjection to the Law and substituted instead a morality of 'do as you please'. He came not to destroy the Law but to fulfil it. He came not to set the Law at naught but to go beyond it. Jesus did not teach men to regard stealing, lying, killing, committing adultery, lightly. Instead he said, in effect: 'You must do more than restrain yourself from killing your enemy, you must love him. You must do more than refrain from stealing another's goods, you must be prepared to share your own with him when he is in need. You must do more than keep yourself from envy of your brother's good fortune, you must, and this is much more difficult, rejoice in it.' Far from despising the Law he showed that Love is the fulfilling of the Law. But before you can go beyond the Law you must begin by respecting it. Love demands not less but more.

It may be that much of the reaction against the preaching of the Law today is, in fact, a reaction against the preaching of legalism, against the suggestion that salvation is to be found through the keeping of certain precepts, through obedience to a certain code, the identification of the Gospel with conventional middle class morality. In so far as the reaction arises out of this it is a healthy reaction, but it is carried too far when it demands the abdication of all responsibility for any form of ethical instruction and substitutes instead the ideal of an 'instant', 'do it yourself' morality. This is naive and fails to take account of the realities of the human situation.

In the actual crisis of temptation no man is capable of a purely rational and objective judgment. We have an infinite capacity for self-deception, for persuading ourselves that what we want to do is what we ought to do. Men are not governed entirely by logic or reason. Emotion plays a very big part in determining their actions and it cannot be assumed that in any given situation their feelings will prove a reliable guide. Failure to realise this is failure to be realistic. The danger of the permissive society, and it is becoming increasingly apparent, is that it fails to inculcate in men and women a respect for law and gives them, in the moment when they are most sorely tempted, no better advice than: "Make up your own mind". Yet it is precisely at this moment that they are least capable of making up their minds. It is at this moment that what stands them in good stead is the fact that they have been taught to respect, honour and obey law.

There may be exceptions to the law, but it is psychologically bad, and morally indefensible, to focus such attention on the exceptions that it undermines the law. For example, you tell your child, 'It is wrong to lie.' You do not, if you are wise, then go on to say, 'But, of course, there are certain extenuating circumstances in which it would be permissible for you to lie.' Because the next time he is tempted to lie he may too easily persuade himself that this is one of these extenuating

29

circumstances. You say, 'Thou shalt not steal.' But do not add, 'Of course were you ever to find yourself in a situation in which the only way to obtain food for a man dying of starvation would be by stealing it; then, in that situation, it would be permissible for you to steal.' It is not necessary to make this kind of qualification because you know that, were he ever to find himself in such a situation, his concern for the life of his fellow man would, rightly, take precedence over everything else.

There is a kind of overscrupulousness which finds its expression in an unwillingness to concede that any law is binding, because there might be some rare exception to it. Human nature is such that it will tend to emphasise the importance of the exception to the detriment of the general principle; and human nature is also such that each individual will be encouraged to regard his case as one of the special cases. Legalism is wrong: but the Law is to be preached since again and again it spells out for us the implications of Love. It may not make men loving, but if they are loving it will guide them in their actions; and if they are not loving, it may encourage them to act in a loving way which can itself help to create love. Let me underline my impression that, in the kind of society in which we are living, there is a genuine danger that preachers seek a spurious reputation for honesty, tolerance, erudition by undermining the Law in the name of the Gospel; by focusing attention upon the exceptions, which are extremely rare, and using them to create a distrust of the general truth. It is no part of the preacher's task to remove the ancient landmarks.

Never in any former age have people been so contemptuous of authority, so impatient of restraint, so insistent upon what they call their freedom, so restive under any kind of discipline. Yet there has never been an age in which freedom was more dangerous, or one in which discipline was more necessary. This can be illustrated from every realm of life: in international relationships where a careless step could plunge the world into suicidal war; in industry where the need for a stricter discipline increases as machines become more complex and even the materials used become more dangerous; on the highways where the mounting slaughter underlines the need for discipline as over and against the freedom of men to drive as fast as they choose, how they choose, and in whatever state of sobriety or insobriety they may happen to be. Even our homes have been made more dangerous by mechanical and electrical devices; and the need to observe rules and take precautions is made unmistakably plain by the staggering total of accidents in the home.

In the realm of morality we see this same need for discipline. The old sanctions which used to operate against promiscuity and infidelity no longer have the same power. Fear of having an illegitimate child can be removed by using the pill. Fear of venereal disease is reduced by the promise that penicillin will cure it. All this means that, if something close to moral chaos is to be avoided, there must be a greater, not a lesser, degree of discipline. It would be tragic if in this situation the preacher failed to make it plain that the people of God are a people set under authority, that there is a discipline which they must accept for themselves and for the good of all men.

Yet we must never preach the Law without the Gospel. To do this may either provoke men to a greater revolt or drive them into a deeper despair. The conclusion of the matter is to be found in the words of the writer of the Epistle of John: "This is the love of

31

God that we keep his commandments: and his commandments are not burdensome."

Words are Suspect.

This is an age in which there is widespread suspicion of, and cynicism about, language, about the words men use. In the more unscrupulous forms of advertising, for example, claims made for various products are not only exaggerated, they are often blatantly, shamelessly and quite deliberately false. When I make this point, it is frequently said that I am foolish to be upset by this kind of thing. It is, so people tell me, all part of the game. The claims are so obviously and so picturesquely untrue that they deceive nobody. No one is expected to take them seriously and, therefore, they do no harm since those who read them are not nearly as gullible as I apparently think they are! I reserve the right to doubt this: but even if it is true that people are not so easily 'taken in', this kind of justification merely makes the whole situation worse. It implies that we are all involved in a conspiracy to make words mean nothing: to pretend that lies are not lies if men do not believe in them and are not taken in by them. It debases and devalues that which is one of the greatest and the most specifically human of our gifts, language.

I think it would be correct to say of a great number of political speeches that they are no longer expected to mean what they say. Indeed, whole armies of political commentators are employed to interpret for us what the leaders of the world really mean when they give utterance. This cynicism about what men say has infected politics to a dangerous degree.

In international affairs it is almost a platitude to say that men no longer understand one another. They may use the same words, but they do not mean the same things. When Russia speaks about Democracy, this is not what we mean by Democracy, or what South Africa means, or India, or Ghana. Countries often have two sets of propaganda, one for internal consumption, one for external consumption; but through mass media people now hear both. There is a radical breakdown in communication between men because of this suspicion of words, of language. Clearly this must affect the preacher, for the suspicion extends to what he has to say.

I began by saying that I do not know the answer. I have only two suggestions and these I leave with you. First, as preachers we must have an awesome respect and reverence for the truth in word and speech. The colourful rhetoric which, at times, has characterised the pulpit in the past, even if it be sincere, has no place today. Second, today the claims made by the Church *must* be illustrated and illumined by the life of the Church.

III

THE PREACHER'S TECHNIQUES

In the discussion of techniques there are two major perils. The impression may be given that preaching is simply a matter of 'know how', of mastering a particular technique. In Acts 19 is recorded the fascinating incident of the magicians of Ephesus. These were men who believed that religion was concerned essentially with the exercise of the correct technique by which the power of God could be used. They were professionals; men who went around claiming that they could drive out evil spirits, heal diseases, predict the future, provide charms which would ward off disaster, bring success in business, marriage, childbirth and in every other realm of human life and activity. They were, of course, paid for their services. They had seen the astonishing works done by Paul and his friends and were both impressed and envious. These Christians had discovered a valuable trade secret which, in the right hands, their own, could prove a veritable gold mine! So they watched, noted and proceeded to copy their methods! They saw that every great work performed by the apostle and his followers was done 'in the name of Jesus'. They knew that the name of the God was very important and therefore would say to patients or customers: 'We adjure you by the Jesus whom Paul preaches'. Thus we have the remarkable, and ironic, spectacle of Jewish exorcists using the name of Jesus as part of their magic rites. It might appear that they were almost ludicrously naive and simple; basically however their error was little different from that of many highly sophisticated men and women of our time. They believed that religion was essentially a matter of technique. The right technique!

34

THE PREACHER'S TECHNIQUES

This has become one of the catch-phrases of the age in which we live. There are thousands of experts whose function is to instruct us on the right techniques, and there is apparently no area of human life which may not be conquered if only we can master the 'right technique'. There are books on the techniques of marriage, friendship, how to win friends and influence people, how to be a good parent, how to be a success in business, how to be healthy, how to be happy, how to be wise. All of us, to a greater or lesser degree, are in danger of succumbing to this idolatry of the technique. In one of his books, Koestler quotes from a lecture given by a party instructor to a literary circle of workmen in a Soviet factory on the production of poetry:

> 'To regard poetry as a special talent which some men possess and others don't is a bourgeois metaphysic. Poetry, like any other skill, is acquired by learning and practice. We need more class-conscious proletarian poetry; we must increase our poetry out-put on the literary front. Beginners should start with five or ten lines a day and then set themselves a target of twenty or thirty lines and gradually increase the quantity and quality of their productions.'

I do not know what effect the prospect of 'more class-conscious proletarian poetry' thus produced has upon you; but I cannot say I view it with any great pleasure. This, surely, is the *reductio ad absurdum* of the worship of techniques. To imagine that the one thing needful is to develop the correct technique is to indulge in magic, in the search for a magic formula which will guarantee success: and there is none.

No less to be avoided is the second major peril: that of despising techniques, the pretence that we are not professionals, the pride of 'sham amateurism', the assumption that we can, to use the phrase attributed to Denney, 'substitute inspiration for perspiration'. Some mistakenly regard it as evidence of a genuine spirituality to go into the pulpit unprepared; and confuse their rambling, disjointed discourses with the inspiration of the Holy Spirit. They reveal scant respect for those who listen to them and may provoke in their listeners scant respect for the intelligence of the Holy Spirit. There is a real sense in which preaching is a trade to be learned; communication, an art to be studied. If a man believes that what he has to say is of paramount importance, he must be prepared to study how to say it in ways which can be understood. 'Born preachers' are rare. For most preaching is a craft to be learnt and demands hard work.

Some years ago, a commercial television company arranged a series of courses to help ministers to use the new medium of communication effectively. I attended the first of these courses. It was interesting and informative: but in one of the sessions in which we were being addressed by a well-known television personality, he made the following statement: 'It is very important that you should be sincere and that people should see that you are sincere, but of course you have to ham it up a bit to be sure that people know that you are sincere.' He could hardly have said anything more calculated to confirm the worst suspicions of those who felt that there was no need for ministers to be instructed in how to use television, and that the suggestion that they needed instruction was a slur, not on their intelligence, but on their integrity, since it implied a willingness on their part to learn a new way of manipulating people. In other words, the basic intention of the course was dishonest. Nothing could have been more unfair to the sponsors of this project than to attribute such motives to them. The fact is that ministers do need to learn how to use television effectively and it is arrogance to deny this. On the other hand 'to ham it up a bit' in order to 'get the message across' is to become a castaway. I quote this incident to illustrate both the danger of idolising the technique and the danger of denying its importance. We have to learn preaching and yet must never imagine that this is all that is involved in preaching.

Where to Begin.

Sunday follows Sunday with relentless regularity and often, it seems, with alarming speed; and on Sundays most of us have to preach twice. I calculate that the average length of a sermon is somewhere around two thousand five hundred words. So that for each Sunday you have to write about five thousand words. Allowing for holidays and exchanges of pulpit this will mean over two hundred thousand words each year. This is a very rough estimate and takes no account of addresses given to children, Bible Classes, Youth Fellowships, Woman's Guilds and other occasions on which a minister may be called to speak. It is a formidable, almost frightening output. How is it to be done? How can one keep it up over the years?

The surest road to mental and spiritual bankruptcy is to leave sermon preparation until Saturday evening and then begin to search desperately for something to say. This is evidence of a failure to recognise the importance of the task with which you have been entrusted. It may be that you will begin writing only on Saturday evening. There are men who cannot bring themselves to put pen to paper until the very last moment, who work best when under pressure: but you should have begun to work at and prepare sermons much earlier in the week, thinking about them, taking notes, reading, planning. I would suggest that you endeavour to begin your preparation on Tuesday and, for myself, I aim to have my two sermons completed by Friday and, except on very rare occasions, they are.

The first essential is to know the Bible, to keep reading it and studying it, not simply as a source book for texts, but as the book in which is to be found the Word of God; that Word whose servant you are and by which you must yourself live. In the course of this reading and study you will find again and again that certain texts and passages lay hold upon you and demand that you preach from them: but something much more important happens, the more you become immersed in the Bible the more you see things, as it were, through the Bible, the more you interpret life in Biblical terms. The Bible is the preacher to the preacher and no other book, however erudite, can be a substitute for it.

Most books on preaching which I have read are very outspoken in their condemnation of 'topical preaching'. I would wish to enter a rider against this general condemnation. If by topical preaching these writers mean the practice of first searching for a topic and then using a concordance to find a text which will fit it, I would endorse their condemnation. This method, if method it may be called, almost inevitably leads to a man imposing his meaning upon the Bible instead of allowing the Bible to make its meaning plain. His ideas may be Biblically sound, but all too often they could not honestly be derived from the passage which he has chosen to expound: and one of the most serious by-products of this is the damaging effect it may have on the way in which ordinary members of the congregation think of the Bible. When they hear the preacher drawing great eternal truths, and they may indeed be great eternal truths, from some rather outré and unpromising text which certainly did not contain them in the first place, they may admire his cleverness and say to themselves: 'I could never have found that message there. If this is how the Bible is to be read it is not for me.'

I once heard a most eloquent sermon on the text 'It came to pass'. The preacher spoke of all the things in life which come to pass; the sorrows and the joys, the pains and the pleasures, the triumphs and the tragedies, youth and age. All, he pointed out with ample illustration, come to pass. It was very interesting. It was often very moving. But it was not preaching from the Bible.

My fear is that this kind of preaching will discourage the average man from reading the Bible. It makes it appear far too esoteric a book to tackle.

Still on 'topical preaching'. There are many occasions in the life of your people and in the life of your community to which you feel you ought to speak, and if you are steeped in the Bible you will find certain passages of scripture come to mind as particularly relevant. I can see nothing wrong in turning to them. Indeed it would seem to be an abdication of responsibility when some great event has deeply affected the lives, consciences, experiences of your people to ignore it and preach as if nothing had happened; as if the men and women before you were not asking; "Is there any word from the Lord about...this?" In the best sense, preaching ought to be topical, to be aware of the world, of the men and women to whom it is directed.

In general material for preaching should arise out of a study of the Bible and an observance of the Christian Year. It is encouraging to discover in the Church of Scotland today an increasing awareness of the Christian

Year and by following it one has some assurance that the great central doctrines of the faith are given their place in our preaching. There is much to be said for the use of a lectionary, though I confess that sometimes I feel that some of the suggested passages have only the most tenuous and dubious connections with the festivals to which they are supposedly related. [1]

It may be that your reading suggests a course of sermons. In the past I have found such a series of great value, particularly at the second service. A series has the double merit that one can be collecting material for it over a number of weeks and that it provides a certain obvious continuity which the congregation recognises and appreciates. Each sermon in a series must stand on its own, independent of the others. This is especially necessary today when one cannot assume a continuity of congregation from week to week. Bible Study, the Christian Year followed by means of a lectionary; these are the main sources which will indicate what you have to preach.

In the experience of most ministers, there come terrible black weeks when they seem to be unable to find anything; when they fear they have 'preached themselves out'. You will have to find your way through these with the help of God, as we all do. They may well come in the nature of a warning that you have 'preached yourself out' because you have been preaching your self.

I have discovered that what I have to do at such times is to begin reading one of the Gospels, or an epistle, or a book from the Old Testament and go on reading until something, somehow, somewhere, 'clicks': or turn to a passage or text upon which I have tried,

1 The Calendar and Lectionary produced by the Joint Liturgical Group avoids these difficulties and is to be recommended.

unsuccessfully, to write before. Often I have discovered that this was the day for which it had been waiting.

What Next?

First discover the best, the most accurate, translation of the text or passage chosen. There are excellent commentaries which will enable one to do this. Make commentaries a first priority when buying books; they are essential — other books can follow. On consulting your commentary, you may find that what you had taken to be the meaning is not the meaning and be tempted to ignore the commentary and to preach on a mistranslation. This is a form of dishonesty which must be resisted. What do the words mean? What did they mean in the context in which originally they were written? What do they mean in the light of God's revelation in Christ for the people to whom on Sunday you will be speaking? It may not be necessary to reveal all this background work to the congregation. As Maltby has said: 'The well is deep and you must have something to draw with but there is no need to make people drink out of the bucket, still less to chew the rope.' It is essential, however, that the preacher undertake this preliminary study.

Be Clear.

Unless you are clear in your own mind about what you want to say it is unlikely that anyone else will understand you. It is not essential always to break a sermon up into three points, to feed your people with a three pronged fork. But a sermon ought to have a definite structure and the bones should be visible. You ought to be able to summarise it in two or three succinct sentences. This need for clarity can hardly be over-emphasised, but it is something which is achieved only as a result of considerable labour. A sermon is not an essay. It is not to be read but to be heard. What may have taken eight hours to prepare has to be absorbed instantaneously. If people are reading an essay or an article and the thought is difficult to follow they can, should they lose the thread of the argument, turn back a page or two and pick it up again. This is not possible when they are listening to a sermon. What you say must be said in such a way that they can grasp it while you are speaking. This means that you must practise to be plain in your thought, and this not at the cost of being shallow; clarity of thought and clarity of expression! Long involved sentences with complicated parentheses, however carefully and lovingly constructed, must be eschewed. The congregation will have lost track before you reach the end of such a sentence. Language and construction which may be acceptable, even admirable, in something meant to be read are often quite unsuitable for preaching. This is one of the problems raised in the writing of sermons. Nevertheless I find it necessary to write mine: though this is a practice which may not commend itself to all. It helps me to clarify my thoughts and is a discipline which I require. My method is, once the initial and basic work on the passage has been done, to sketch out a skeleton of the sermon. I then write it out long hand and I may do this twice, even three times. Then I type it, and, while doing so, tend to speak each sentence so that what emerges is something which, I hope, sounds right for preaching. To many this may seem an over laborious and over meticulous way of doing things, and for many it would be; but for me it is necessary because I am neither a quick writer nor a fluent speaker. It takes me a long time to prepare a sermon but, having typed the final draft, I then know what I am going to say. I probably spend a Saturday morning mulling over Sunday's sermons and then preach them, usually without reference to the manuscript. I do not suggest that everyone should adopt this method. It simply happens to be the one which suits me, and each of you will have to discover his own method.

Be Concrete.

Be specific rather than general. I recall hearing the story of a little community in Canada which was situated on the banks of a river a few miles downstream from a large lumber camp. The people in this village were in the habit of fishing logs out of the river as they floated down after felling. They then sawed off the ends, which bore the lumber company's stamp, and used the logs to build houses and barns. Now a new minister came to the community and was rather shocked at the existence of this clearly dishonest practice among his flock. So one Sunday he preached a sermon on the commandment: 'Thou shalt not steal'. At the end of the service he stood at the door of the church while the congregation filed past him. The members shook hands with him and murmured nice things about the service; what a splendid sermon it had been; how much that kind of thing needed to be said these days; how completely they were in agreement with him. But it did not seem to have gone home, his shots appeared to have missed their target, for the people continued, as before, to remove the lumber company's logs from the river. The following Sunday he took as his text: 'Thou shalt not cut the ends off other people's logs' — and they ran him out of town! They were not disturbed by his generalisations. It was when he became specific that they reacted. Sermons compounded of vague generalisations and comfortable abstractions are not likely to disturb or affect anyone.

The Use of Illustrations.

Do not hesitate to use illustrations but use them wisely. This means use them sparingly, and be sure that they are apt.

There are sermons so overloaded with illustrations that the cutting edge of them is completely blunted and people remember only a collection of little stories. There is a real pitfall here! Few can resist the temptation to find a place somehow for a good illustration when we come across one. It burns a hole in one's pocket and it is very difficult to keep it for use at the right time. The best illustrations are those which are drawn from life, and the worst are the kind to be found in books with such titles as *The Thousand Best Sermon Illustrations.* All too often these are far too slick and easy, and often too sentimental.

Let me give you an example of one which was going the rounds when I was a student and which I was interested to find quoted in one of Dr. Paul Scherer's sermons — quoted, I need hardly say, with marked disapproval. The picture is of a storm at sea. Out from the shore there is a ship in distress. On the beach the lifeboat crew are preparing to launch their boat. Around them a group of people is gathered. Suddenly an elderly woman detaches herself from the little crowd and, throwing her arms around a member of the lifeboat crew — a young man — she cries: 'Don't go out, John! Don't go out! Your father was lost at sea in just such a storm as this. Your brother Willie has not been heard of for over a year now, and I am fearing that he has gone too. Don't go out! You are all I have left! Please, John!' But John, gently freeing himself from her grip, says:

'Don't you understand, Mother? We must go out! It doesn't matter if we come back!' So far so good; and so far credible, just! But the story goes on! The lifeboat thrusts its way through the stormy seas, sometimes disappearing in them, out to the wounded ship. The watchers on the shore see it reach the ship, take men off and then begin to pull back to the shore again. As it comes nearer they can distinguish John standing in the bow, his hands cupped to his mouth. He is shouting something. They listen intently and, at last, above the fury of the wind and the crash of the breakers, they hear his words: 'Tell mother, Willie's here!' Paul Scherer makes the comment: 'It was a good story — too good!'

I have to confess that this kind of illustration makes me feel slightly sick. Perhaps the story is true, but it certainly does not ring true. It is far too pat, too easy, too tidy. Life is not like this and people know that. Beware of the slick, too perfect, illustration!

Be careful too, when you use illustrations taken from some field of knowledge with which you are not familiar, that you get your facts correct. Once, in the course of a sermon, I happened to mention the number of chromosomes we inherit; and I had hardly reached the vestry before I was informed that I was one out. There are always people like this, who seem to be waiting to pounce upon a slip. This should not worry you. But where you do, through carelessness, make some grotesque error in fact, it is serious. Many a sixth form schoolboy in your congregation may know more science than you do. If you make some obvious blunder concerning the things he does know, he will regard with suspicion the other things you have to say. You cannot be an expert in every field of knowledge; but, if you are going to illustrate from some particular field with which you are not familiar, make sure that you check your information: not to save your own pride, but because inaccuracy here may have a damaging effect upon the credibility of the rest of your message.

Do not be Dull.

It is a cardinal sin for a preacher to be dull. Any man speaking on something which really matters to him, and which he wants me to understand, can capture my attention. His subject may be anything from his job to some absorbing hobby. If he is interested in it himself, and eager that I should know about it, he will hold my attention. How then is it possible for us to be dull? We have to share with men the best of all good tidings, to declare a Gospel which is directed to all men and women, which concerns the whole of life? It is the most damning criticism if people should dismiss what we say as dull! It means either that we ourselves are not excited, thrilled, obsessed by the importance of what we have to say, or that we do not care sufficiently about men and women to make the effort to convey our meaning in terms which they can understand. If the preacher is not passionately convinced about the need to make men hear his message it is little wonder that others ignore it. Dullness is primarily the result of dull minds, dull souls. People may not agree with you. They may even resent what you have to say: but they should not be able to ignore it. Any man with any real sensitivity must be aware when he is boring his congregation, and he will then ask himself not, 'What is wrong with them?' but, 'What is wrong with me?' The dullness is not in the message itself but in the way in which it is communicated. The fundamental fault is a lack of sensitivity, a lack of awareness of the people to whom one is speaking.

We are often warned not to preach above people's heads. The warning may be justified; and, if it is, it usually means either that we are not sufficiently clear in our own minds what we are trying to say, or that we do not know enough about the lives, the language, the interests of those whom we are addressing. It may be a combination of both, but the result is dullness!

No less a danger is that of talking down to a congregation, of wearying them with dreary platitudes and painstaking pedestrianism. C. E. Montague, in *A Writer's Notes on His Trade*, caricatures the kind of verbal prolixity which can drive a congregation to take refuge in sleep or inattention. He writes, 'You must at sometime or other have groaned dumbly under a flood of dearness from the pulpit. First the giving out of a text, clear as noon, perhaps the words, 'A city that is set on a hill.' Then the illumination of this heavenly lamp by setting out, all round it, pound after pound of tallow candles. From word to word of the text the hapless divine straggles onward, matchbox in hand: "A city, mark you! Not two cities. Not twin cities like Assisi and Perugia, each set on its Umbrian hill. Not one of these potent leagues of cities which shine in the storied page of history like constellations in the natural firmament. And yet a city; no mere village! No hamlet perched on a knoll as the traveller may see them in the Apennines...." And so on and on until the martyred Christian below has to ask in his heart, "Shall I never hit back!"'

It is not needful to indulge in gimmickry or pulpit pyrotechnics to avoid being dull. All that is necessary is that a preacher should feel the importance of what he has to say, sufficiently to study to say it well, and in a language which those who listen will be able to understand.

Do not Overload.

Many of us try to say too much. Professor Mackintosh used to warn his students against this fault by pointing out that a sermon which is overloaded is like a pipe which has been too tightly packed with tobacco. It 'will not draw'. And he would add; 'When a pipe is packed too tightly, it is usually filled with someone else's tobacco!'

To Read or not to Read.

There are men who read their sermons and hold one's attention without any difficulty. There are others who have an almost fatal fluency which enables them to preach 'without paper' and sometimes, one gets the impression, almost without thinking! I find it extremely difficult to read a sermon. I am temperamentally incapable of this. I must look at people when I am speaking to them, and if I cannot see them I begin to be oppressed by a growing conviction that they are not listening. They may sometimes not be listening even when I am looking at them, but this is beside the point. One famous preacher used to speak of 'preaching with the eye'. I know what he meant. All my senses are quickened and sharpened when I am preaching. I see people with greater distinctness. I can detect the least movement. I know when they are beginning to shift restlessly in their seats. I think I know when they are listening and when they have 'switched off'. I need to see them and speak to them. Thus, for me, the method is to prepare my sermon in such a way that I know clearly what I am going to say and, though I carry my manuscript with me into the pulpit, I rarely use it except for quotations. The sermon, as preached, is very much as I have written it though words here and there may be altered and I may change an illustration in 'mid

THE PREACHER'S TECHNIQUES

stream' as it were. Probably the best method is to use notes: to write your sermon and then reduce it to a page of notes. This may not result in impeccable prose, and the sermon may fall even farther short of being a literary masterpiece, but the gain in freshness and immediacy will more than compensate for any literary inadequacies.

I do not recommend memorising. It imposes a very great strain on the preacher and may well result in his reading his sermon off the back of his mind. It is a fairly useful indication of how clearly you have expressed your thoughts if you can, without recourse to your manuscript, sit back in your chair and follow through the line of your argument. If you find this so difficult as to be impossible, then I question whether your congregation will be able to follow your sermon, hearing it, as they do, for the first time.

There is really no 'best method'. Each individual must work out his own method for himself.

Group Preparation.

In his book *The Humiliation of the Church,* Albert Van den Heuvel has a chapter entitled "Experimental Preaching" in which he suggests that, for the age in which we are living, sermon preparation should be less individualistic and more of a group activity. Horst Symanowski in his *The Christian Witness in an Industrial Society* makes a similar plea, and reports on experiments which he has, himself, conducted on this method. Van den Heuvel writes:

> 'The congregation is split into well mixed groups of about fifteen people. These groups rotate the preaching ministry. Early in the week the group comes together with the minister. They listen to an exegesis of the passage and meditate silently

49

afterwards for about half an hour. Then all share their insights and their questions. Finally a group decision is made on the most important questions. The preacher, either the minister or a layman, is responsible for the final draft. Of course he has the freedom to say that the group never came to the heart of the matter; but, whether he agrees or disagrees, the voice of the whole congregation is heard on Sunday.' [1]

There are certain fairly obvious criticisms one could make of this experiment. It is, for example, questionable whether, in the kind of group one would be able to assemble for this purpose, the voice of the whole congregation would be heard. I have a suspicion that the voice might well be the voice of a comparatively small, articulate and probably intellectual minority.

It is also open to question whether it is the voice of the congregation which should be heard on Sunday! These objections aside, there is value in this suggestion and, with certain modifications, it might well be worth trying.

An experiment on similar lines was, in fact, carried out in 'The Word for Living' series broadcast on the B.B.C. some years ago. In these, a group of people studied a passage of scripture and then tried to live with it throughout the following week. They afterwards reported on their experiences, which the minister then tried to gather up in a sermon.

Any minister, who has had a Bible Study Group in his congregation, would be able to testify how much it can influence his sermon preparation; how helpful it can be in the insights it provides into the lives of men and women. Though here again, there is a danger of

1 *The Humiliation of The Church,* Albert H. Van den Heuvel, S.C.M. Press, London, 1967, p 72.

forgetting that the Bible Study Group is not necessarily representative of the congregation, and may give a false picture of the congregation as a whole. Provided that one is aware that there are these dangers, I have no doubt that there are real possibilities in this kind of group work which should be explored.

The idea of ministers doing a certain amount of their sermon preparation in groups is one which has always had a considerable attraction for me though I have had little experience of it; and such experiences as I have had have tended to be fortuitous rather than the result of deliberate planning. I see nothing against, and much to be said for, local ministers meeting regularly to study, let's say, the passage provided in the lectionary; and, in a very general way, to plan their sermons together. This would not result in identical sermons being preached in all the neighbourhood churches. We are much too individualistic for this to happen. Perhaps we are much too individualistic for this kind of experiment; too determined that we should be able to say of our sermons; 'All my own work'. If this be so, we may need to be reminded that the Holy Spirit appears to have a preference for working in groups and fellowships.

I have tried to emphasise the need to take seriously the learning of the craft of preaching. I have tried to deal with some of the practicalities of sermon preparation, and I have hinted at new possibilities for experiment. The essential message remains the same. The language in which it is couched, the techniques of communication, vary, and must vary from age to age, and we should always be open to the need for experiment, as we should always be willing to face the fact of our failure in communication, and to ask why, and how it may be corrected.

IV

PREACHING AND THE MASS MEDIA
(RADIO AND TELEVISION)

No study which purports to deal with the subject of the communication of the Gospel in the modern world can afford to ignore the part played by Radio and Television. They provide opportunities but also have a powerful influence upon the habits, the thinking, the ethos of the majority of men and women in our country. If, in the first instance, one considers not specifically religious television but television in general, it would be foolish to deny that it has a very considerable influence upon the religious scene.

There are many people who avoid being out on certain evenings and do not welcome visitors because they have a regular 'date' with 'Coronation Street', 'Till Death Do Us Part', 'Meet The Wife', 'The Big Valley', or whatever, at the moment, happens to be the series to which they are particularly addicted. When Celtic played Inter-Milan in the final of the European Cup the streets of Glasgow were as empty and deserted as they are on a wet Sunday afternoon.

All manner of small local societies having semi-cultural aims, literary societies, philosophical societies, musical societies have been drastically affected by the advent of television and many of them have found it impossible to continue in being. Even the public houses have, in many cases, been forced to install television sets to meet the demands of their customers. The fact is that a considerable number of people today have formed 'viewing habits'. They watch certain programmes at certain times and they arrange their leisure to allow them to do this. Many church members are to be found in this category. The faithful few may still attend an evening service but quite a number of them rush back home as quickly as possible because they 'always watch Dr. Finlay's Casebook' on Sunday evenings. It is not unreasonable to conclude that television has hastened the demise of many evening services. Moreover it has succeeded in doing this without unduly disturbing the conscience of those who formerly attended such services, since it provides a religious programme which coincides, roughly, with the hour of the second service and thereby enables people to tell themselves that, even if they have not been to church, they have, at least, shared in an act of worship, a religious service of some kind! Television is not solely responsible for the decline in the second service, but it is one factor which has quickened the rate of that decline. On the credit side it must be borne in mind that television has encouraged a number of people who never attended an evening service, and never had any intention of doing so, to devote at least part of their attention on a Sunday evening to matters concerning the faith.

But television does more than effect changes in habits and time-tables, it also influences thinking, affects one's way of looking at the world. It does this, whether one is conscious of being influenced or not, and whether one is a church member or not. The war in Vietnam, with all its horror, its cruelty, its tragedy comes right into your living room. The racial riots in America explode in front of your eyes. The victims of the landslide, or the earthquake, are dug out of the ground while you watch. There is an immediacy about it all which is both horrifying and, in a macabre way, fascinating. Men are killed or wounded, women weep over their dead children, and you see it as it is happening.

The effect of this television coverage of real events is bound to be different from the effect created by reading reports in newspapers, or even of looking at newsreel pictures shown several days after the events have occurred. We have not yet discovered what this effect is. Does it promote a deeper compassion and concern? Or, because it comes out of that little square box, on which, only a moment before, you were being entertained by some irrelevant frivolity, does it lose its power, so that reality itself, in its cruelest, saddest, most tragic manifestations, becomes just another form of entertainment? Through television reporting, men have been made conscious, as never before, of the sheer burden of suffering and tragedy in the world. May this produce in some not compassion but, as a kind of defence mechanism, a dullness, almost a callousness, concerning human grief, pain and misery? May it produce in others anger, the anger of helplessness and frustration? I recall a friend telling me, how, during the war, the unit to which he was attached moved up to the outskirts of a little village near Lake Trasimeno in Italy. The village had been bombed and shelled and there was hardly one stone left standing upon another. It did not seem possible that anyone could still be living there. The men began to prepare their evening meal and, while they were thus engaged, there emerged from the rubble and the ruins of the shattered village little groups of men, women and children. They formed a circle round the soldiers. They said nothing. They asked for nothing. They just stood there and watched. It was all too obvious that they were desperately hungry. The soldiers gave to them the food which they had been preparing. It was not enough. They gave them all the food they had. It was not enough. Still the people stood there in silence, watching and waiting. In the end the soldiers could bear it no longer and drove them away with curses. When people are constantly exposed to an intolerable situation which they feel powerless to remedy, their reaction may be not concern or compassion but anger. May not this be one of the unforeseen effects of television reporting? To such questions add these: How far do reality and unreality, fact and fiction, become dangerously confused in the minds of the viewers? and, How far does the reporting of certain events produce imitative behaviour on the part of some viewers? It then becomes obvious that there is urgent need for a study in depth of this whole subject. We may then find the answers to some of the questions we ask about what may be regarded as legitimate subjects for treatment on television. One thing is certain, that the events depicted upon that screen are a part of the background, the consciousness of the people who Sunday by Sunday look up from their pews to the man in the pulpit. Consciously or unconsciously, they judge the preacher's message by its relevance, or lack of relevance, to what is happening in this world which television has brought so close to so many of them.

The latest advances in science and medicine, and the peculiar ethical problems which these pose for those who handle them, are given a very wide publicity. They are presented, discussed and debated in the homes of many who would not otherwise have been aware of them or understood them. They may not be, indeed generally they are not, dealt with within the framework of religious faith but they raise problems which religious people cannot ignore, however much, in the past, they have contrived to ignore similar problems.

These things then are part of the awareness of the congregation to which the preacher addresses himself on Sundays at eleven a.m. and six-thirty p.m. and I suspect that we have not yet sufficiently realised this. Even those programmes which might be labelled as 'Light Entertainment' carry certain other important overtones. They may cheapen, or they may elevate taste, make people *more* or *less* sensitive, create new appetites or destroy old ones. To some degree they help to shape, and to some degree they reflect, the culture of ordinary men and women. They project some kind of image of the world and of life to which men and women respond, either by identification or by rejection. They say something about the world of our day and about how people think; and, at the same time, they play their part, great or small, in the making of that world and the shaping of that thinking.

There are, of course, those who would have us believe that what comes out of the television set has no power to influence or alter thinking and opinions. This is a very dangerous illusion to foster. Shrewd business men do not spend large sums of money for advertising time on television without fairly strong evidence that it is a powerfully persuasive medium. Political parties do not haggle for space on television without some justification for believing that it can be used to convince the public of the soundness of their policies. Men and women are influenced by what they see and hear. Those of us who knew Hitler's Germany in the 1930s can testify to the importance of the part played by radio in conditioning the minds of the German people by Nazi propaganda: and those of us who lived through the second world war know how much the morale of the nation was strengthened by the radio speeches of Winston Churchill.

To be able to make men see, as well as hear, is to have enormously increased power. We in the Church should know this. For a long time the Church made use of pictures, pageants, mimes and drama, to reinforce its message. It may be that, with the advent of printing, the 'eye-gate', especially in the Protestant churches, suffered neglect, but there is no room for doubt that today it is, once more, something with which we must reckon. Television is the most important revolution in communication since the invention of printing.

Radio and television together have introduced new factors into the situation in which the preacher of the Gospel now finds himself. They help to create the kind of world to which he speaks. They help form the background to the thinking of the majority of the men and women to whom he speaks. They stimulate a new awareness of all manner of political, social and moral issues which have a profound theological content; and they reveal, and may sometimes pander to, the prejudices and the basic preconceptions of the society in which the Church lives and works, and to which it must witness. The preacher will have to take account of their influence, even if he never conducts a service on the radio or appears in front of a television camera. He would have to take account of their influence even if there were no specifically religious broadcasts or television programmes. Indeed what happens in the so-called secular fields of television is as important, perhaps even more important for him than what happens in what has been designated as 'The Religious Slot'.

Religious Broadcasting.

I wonder whether it is realised how considerable is the volume of religious broadcasting. There will be, on any Sunday, in the region of two hours and twenty minutes of religious television and three and a half hours of religious programmes on sound radio. Each day of the week there is a minimum of thirtyfive minutes given to religion on sound radio, and this does not take into account religious programmes for schools and all the other occasional programmes, talks, interviews, dealing with religious subjects. Television also has its quota of religious programmes during the week, though the number of these will vary from week to week. At a rough estimate, Scotland receives some four hundred and fifty hours of sound broadcasting and some one hundred and eightyfive hours of television devoted to religion in the course of a year, and this takes no account of the special programmes, such as the ten hours of television at the time of the General Assembly of the Church of Scotland, and the number of occasions on which religion is dealt with in news and current affairs programmes. To this must be added the religious programmes which are shown on the Commercial Channels. S.T.V., for example, devotes one and a half hours a week to religious television as a regular practice and also gives space to religious programmes at other times. When one considers the amount of money paid by business firms to advertise their goods for, perhaps, thirty seconds each day, the very considerable cost involved in mounting any television programme, and the fact that in many other countries both radio and T.V. space has to be purchased by the churches at commercial rates, we should consider ourselves very fortunate that all this time is given without cost to the churches.

The opportunities which it presents are enormous. Take the sound radio programme, 'Five to Ten'. It has been calculated that the number of people who listen regularly, that is once or twice every week, to 'Five to Ten' is about fourteen million, or nearly one third of the adult population of the United Kingdom. In addition there are a further eight million who listen occasionally. Admittedly this is one of the most popular religious programmes on sound radio and the figures will not be nearly so high for a morning service. Nevertheless it is a fact that no man ever speaks into a microphone in a studio, or appears in front of a T.V. camera, without addressing far more people on that one occasion than he will ever do at any other time in his life. Indeed, on that one occasion, he may speak to more people than the sum total of those who have attended all the services he has conducted throughout a long ministry. Even those religious programmes which are televised at such a late hour that one may wonder whether there is any viewing public for them, can have an audience which may run to several hundred thousand.

It need hardly be underlined that this great unseen congregation is composed of many different categories of viewers or listeners. There are many church members included in it, and this will be particularly true when church services are broadcast or televised. Of these a fairly large number will be old sick people who, for one reason or another, are housebound and prevented from attending church. I once heard radio services criticised by a minister who pointed out that they were listened to by the sick and the aged only. Even if this were true, it would still be a magnificent ministry of inestimable value and one for which we ought to be very grateful, since surely the old and sick are no less dear to God than the young and healthy. For a very large number of men and women radio and television services are literally God-sends. It is not true, however, that these services are heard, or seen, only by the aged and the sick. In this vast congregation there are also many who are but nominal members of the Church, many who have lapsed or who have only the most tenuous of connections with the Church, many who could be described as being on the fringes of the Christian Faith, and almost certainly some who are right outside it. These last two groups may be more readily reached by programmes which are not direct broadcasts of formal church services. Not all those who disclaim any connection with the churches are hostile to the Christian Faith, and through radio and television we are provided with an unequalled opportunity to reach people who would never come near our churches.

It may well be asked what effect, if any, all this volume of religious broadcasting has, and there are, no doubt, some who would maintain that its effects are minimal; that its influence is of the most ephemeral nature. I am prepared to deny this categorically. Religious broadcasting is 'casting seed' and the parable of the Sower is particularly relevant to it. It has been called by the Rev. Penry Jones 'Breadcasting' — the casting of bread upon the water — and the description is an apt one. It is not possible to produce statistical evidence for what it accomplishes, but then it is equally impossible, despite the multitude of forms and returns with which the minister today is inundated, to produce statistical information about the results achieved by preaching anywhere. Is it not perhaps of God's Grace that this should be so? We might else be tempted to count scalps, and thereafter to take to ourselves a credit which can belong only to God. Yet some evidence there is, given by God for our encouragement, of the fact that some of the seed does fall upon fruitful ground, finds a lodging in the hearts of men and women, takes root, grows and brings forth fruit. Dr. Ronald Falconer, of the Religious Broadcasting Department of the B.B.C., quotes the experience of Professor Barclay that during a television series he has to give up two mornings a week to pastoral phone calls and interviews with people who have contacted him, and this does not take account of the voluminous correspondence with which he has to deal. Many of us remember with gratitude the radio ministry exercised by the Rev. Ronald Selby Wright during the second world war and the widespread response which it elicited.

My own personal experience is not nearly so dramatic and startling as that of many other men but over the years I have been engaged in a fair amount of radio and television work and in every case I have had a recordable, and I stress the word 'recordable', response far beyond anything one normally receives from an ordinary service in one's own church. The reaction has sometimes been hostile; but, setting aside the letters, nice or nasty, which come from the kind of people who feel a compulsion to write to anyone who speaks on radio or appears on television, I have again and again been moved by the people who have written, and have found myself committed to a real pastoral relationship with some of them. 'No one is ever converted by a radio or television broadcast' is the kind of remark one frequently hears when this subject is under discussion. In a sense it is true; but no one is ever converted anywhere or anyhow save by the work of the Holy Spirit, and that the Holy Spirit may, and does, use these media, and that men and women are converted, I have myself no doubt.

The number of those who write letters and make phone calls must constitute a very tiny minority of those who respond to the message. Religious broadcasting is, at least potentially, one of the most powerful agents for evangelism in the modern world. I use the word 'potentially'. It is not nearly as effective as it might be, but neither are we as effective as we might

61

be; and I am sure that those who are responsible for religious broadcasting, those who are professionally involved, are no more complacent about their achievements than we are.

The Use of the Media.

People who come to church do so with a greater or lesser predisposition to listen and willingness to worship. This is by no means true of all those who make up the radio and television audiences. Some, undoubtedly, tune in because they desire to share in an act of worship. Many who listen or view have no such initial intention.

Television and radio are considered to be media largely for entertainment, and this presents problems for both the producers and the presenters of religious programmes. Here there is no captive audience of the kind one has in a church. It is much easier for a man to switch off his radio or television set than it would be for him to walk out in the middle of a church service, however much he might, at times, feel inclined to do so. The need to command attention immediately is, therefore, correspondingly greater, and clearly this must bring with it certain attendant dangers of introducing 'stunts' and 'gimmickry' which have the effect of obscuring the message or making it seem to be of secondary importance. Because one does not know one's audience, one may be tempted to speak down to them, or to attribute to them a higher degree of sophistication than they possess. Nothing demands a greater integrity on the part of the preacher than this medium, where the checks naturally imposed by facing a live congregation of men and women are not usually present; and, even where they are, as in the broadcasting of a church service, are present in a somewhat self-conscious and artificial setting in which people are aware that they are being 'broadcast' or 'televised'. The preparation for any service of this kind, therefore, requires an added spiritual discipline on the part of the preacher, and, if a congregation is present, on the part of the congregation. It demands also a greater degree of sanctified imagination.

Although the preacher may be speaking to a much greater number of people than he ever does in his own congregation, yet it is essential that he should remember that they are not all gathered together in one vast auditorium. On the contrary they are listening in ones and twos and threes in their own homes. He must not address them as if they were a mass-meeting; and what might be natural to a man sitting in a large congregation may seem somehow grotesque when he is sitting at his own fireside. Most of us who are preachers find this a difficult adjustment to make; and I believe it is a form of communication which might well be studied and taught in college, with considerable advantage to the increasing number who, in the future, will be expected to make use of it.

Television is still in its infancy, though it is a fairly robust child, and there is a continuing development in techniques. It would be strange if those engaged in the production of religious television programmes were not conscious of the new developments and eager to discover if, and how, they can be applied to make religious programmes more effective. One can understand the importance and the fascination of this. These men and women may be engaged in the work of the *Religious* Broadcasting Department but they are also professionals who are in constant contact with other professionals working in the same general field of communication through television, and one would expect them to observe and profit from the experience of their colleagues in other departments. But there is a danger here. In putting on a 'show' of some kind it may well be that the form is as important, in some cases more important, than the content. In religious broadcasting the content is, and must always be, supremely important, while the form, obviously, cannot be ignored. From my experience, both of viewing and of taking part in television programmes, I am persuaded that by the very nature of the truths to be communicated, the most effective form of communication will always be that of person to person (note 'person to person' not parson to person) and I have reason to believe that this opinion is shared by some, if not all, of those who are engaged in the production of religious television. In a paper delivered to the European Area Conference of the World Association for Christian Broadcasting, Dr. Falconer had this to say:

> 'When television came to us, a man talking to, or before, a camera was considered 'bad television'. Television had to do with moving pictures, like film, evocative pictures constituting a unity of vision, sound and movement. It was a new art form; something far above a simple means of communication. In 1952 no one had spoken alone in front of a camera for more than seven minutes.'

He then went on to speak of the extraordinary enthusiasm of the response to a series of four programmes in which Professor Barclay talked, preached, lectured, in front of the cameras alone for twentyfive minutes and continued:

> 'Even more exciting was the positive reaction of agnostics... It almost seemed as if the agnostics were exposed for the first time to a preacher totally caught up in his subject, who obviously loved people and could communicate to them in terms they

understood. When I watched him at work I had an uncomfortable feeling that if we had begun here twelve years ago we might have used our time to greater advantage.'

If the truth we communicate is personal and is communicated through a person then one can understand why this 'person to person' confrontation has proved to be so effective and impressive.

Religious Broadcasting and the Churches.

The Aim of Religious Broadcasting as stated in the B.B.C. handbook for 1963 is:

'The aims of religious broadcasting may be briefly summarised under three heads. The first is that it should reflect the worship, thought, and action of these churches which represent the main stream of the Christian Tradition in the country. The second is that religious broadcasting should bring before listeners and viewers what is most significant in the relationship between the Christian Faith and the modern world. The third aim is that religious broadcasting should seek to reach those on the fringe of the organised life of the churches or quite outside it.'

My contention would be that it is just because religious broadcasting does, all too accurately, reflect the worship, thought and action of the churches that it so often fails to reach those on the fringe of the organised life of the churches, or quite outside it. For the great majority of those who occupy this position of being on the fringe of the churches' life, or outside it, the only image of the Church which they have is the one they receive through religious broadcasting, and that image is all too faithful.

65

This is borne out by the project conducted by the William Temple College on 'Mainstream Religion — A Study of the Content of Religious Programmes during the month of June 1963'.

The method employed was as follows.

Reports were made on almost every religious programme presented by the B.B.C. and the Independent Television Companies during that month. At the same time reports were made on the Sunday services in twentythree churches of various denominations and in various parts of the country. By offering a comparison with the broadcasts these reports gave some indication as to how far the latter can be accurately described as reflecting the worship, thought and tradition of these churches which represent the mainstream of the Christian tradition in the country. The conclusion reached in this report was a very significant one. It ran:

> 'The picture of Christianity presented by the broadcasts and church services agree to a very large extent. The only adequate explanation of this is that they are both drawn from the common stock of Christian teaching and worship; this is the sort of thing that most Christian preachers are in fact saying today; this is the sort of worship that is going on in most churches... The Church on the screen is all of a piece with the church or chapel round the corner.' [1]

In other words, Religious Broadcasting in general reflects the Church as it is, and inevitably reveals its weakness and its failures. Thus the weakness and the failures of Religious Broadcasting are the weakness and failures of the churches. It cannot and could not be otherwise. If it is right that Religious Broadcasting

1 *Mainstream Religion,* William Temple College, Corby.

should reflect mainstream religion, the worship, action and life of the churches, and they would, I suspect, be the first to object if it did not, then we must accept that it is bound to reflect also the failings, the shortcomings, the inadequacies of the churches. In this connection it is worth noting some of the criticisms made of mainstream religion in this report since we may learn from them.

1. The Church is greatly preoccupied with itself. From half to one-third of the sermons are about the Church. About half the prayers are on behalf of the Church. This far outweighs any other concern.

2. The Church sees itself as called upon to be the servant of the world, to care for the outcasts of society particularly. The frequency of exhortations to do this may spring from the fact that preachers feel this is not what their congregations are actually doing. It may also spring from uneasiness about how the Church can find a useful role to play in society... In other words it may be another form of the Church's preoccupation with itself.

3. This desire to serve the world is off-set by a lack of awareness as to what is actually going on there.

4. This unawareness seems to be part of a general lack of contact with reality. National and international events are rarely important unless they impinge upon some aspect of life which the Church has taken over as its own province. Local life goes on unremarked. The importance of industry in British society goes almost unrecognised.

5. There is between Broadcast Religion and that of the Churches the same attitude towards the Bible. Its importance is stressed. It is greatly

used in worship but seldom as a stimulus to thought or as something which requires some effort of understanding. It is used rather as an aid to establishing a devotional mood or atmosphere, or to make whatever point the preacher or speaker has already decided to make.

It has to be noted that, although the survey did include Scotland, it was not wide enough, nor were the samples taken numerous enough, to give a very accurate picture of the situation in Scotland and it might be argued that the report reflects the English scene more nearly than the Scottish one. It would be very foolish of Scottish churchmen to indulge the illusion that things are very different in Scotland. I believe that most of the criticisms are applicable to both countries. Thus it must be concluded that if Religious Broadcasting is to reflect the mainstream religion in our country, is to reflect the life, thought, action and worship of the churches, its effectiveness as an instrument of evangelism will be proportionate to the effectiveness of the churches.

It is important that the relationship between the churches and Religious Broadcasting should continue to be a close one. If Religious Broadcasting ceases to reflect the mainstream religion of the churches then it will not only fail to minister to the large numbers of church members who, for one reason or another, are unable to attend public worship, it will also be in danger of creating a vague amorphous 'T.V. Church' to add to the already too numerous list of sects and denominations. I use the word 'church' in quotation marks for whatever else it may be it cannot be, in any true sense, a church; for it will be without sacraments, without discipline, without fellowship or any corporate witness, without any genuine outlet of service to the community. Yet the adherents of this artificially created group may well regard it as a substitute for church membership and an adequate reason for not committing themselves to any organisational church.

On the other hand, it is important that Religious Broadcasting should not be so closely tied to the established churches that all experimentation is stultified by the protest; "This does not reflect the norm". Our norm is not so unqualifiedly successful that we can dare claim it to be beyond criticism or improvement. It may well be that Religious Broadcasting, covering as it does a much wider spectrum of society than the churches, can supply insights and experiences which could be of inestimable value to our understanding of the means by which the Gospel is to be communicated to the world.

The churches can serve Religious Broadcasting by making sure that it does not fall into the hands of an esoteric elite who could easily be more out of touch with the real world of men and women than is the average parish minister. Religious Broadcasting can serve the churches by revealing to us, the preachers, weaknesses which are far more devastatingly delineated by exposure to a television audience than to the captive audience of a congregation; by a willingness to experiment in new methods and forms of communication which might well be resisted by the average congregation were they to come from their own minister; by encouraging the kind of dialogue with the world which cannot easily be conducted within the context of a traditional service of worship.

All this will demand a readiness on the part of both ministers and congregations to welcome such experimentation and not to insist that Religious Broadcasting should at all times merely reproduce what happens in the average parish church Sunday by Sunday. We must be willing to allow a considerable measure of freedom to those who are concerned with the production of religious programmes. We must understand that the kind of approach which is approved and applauded by those within the churches may often seem quite meaningless to those outside.

I have said nothing about the personality of the preacher and the dangers to which he is exposed when he becomes involved in radio and television work since these are only variations or extensions of the dangers which are inherent in being a preacher.

One word of warning. We must, at all costs, avoid the attitude which considers an invitation to conduct a service on radio or television as a desirable 'status symbol' either for the minister or the congregation, and should shun, like the plague, the envy which expresses itself in such comments as, 'Why should they be on again?'

Much has still to be discovered about the use of television, but I am certain it is potentially a most powerful instrument for evangelism. It is, also and inevitably, going to expose the Church in increasing measure to the cool, sometimes hostile, sometimes wistful, even hopeful, scrutiny of the vast numbers of men and women outside it.

We can learn from it. We can cooperate with it. We can use it. We can abuse it. The opportunities are great and, as one would expect, so are the dangers. The one thing we dare not do is ignore it.

V

THE PREACHER'S PERSONALITY

The pulpit is a dangerous place. Preaching, like marriage, is, in the words of the *Book of Common Order,* "not to be entered upon lightly or unadvisedly, but thoughtfully, reverently and in the fear of God, and with due consideration of the ends for which it was ordained."

Phillips Brooks' often quoted definition of preaching as 'Truth through Personality' has sometimes been savagely criticised as encouraging the cult of personality. Wrenched out of its context it could be thus interpreted, but this does less than justice to Brooks. He did not, as his detractors have sometimes suggested, exaggerate the importance of personality at the expense of the sovereignty of truth. He was insistent that the preacher is a messenger; and wrote:

'I think that nothing is more needed to correct the peculiar vices of preaching which belong to our time than a new prevalence among preachers of this first conception of the truth which they have to tell as a message. I am sure that one of the great sources of weakness of the pulpit is the feeling among the people that these men who stand up before them every Sunday have been making up trains of thought and thinking how they should 'treat' their subject, as the phrase runs. This is the first ground of the vicious habit that our congregations have of talking about the preacher more than they talk about the truth. The minstrel, who sings before you to show his skill, will be praised for his wit and rhymes and voice. But the courier, who hurries in breathless to bring you a message, will be forgotten in the message that he brings.'[1]

1 *Lectures on Preaching,* Phillips Brooks, S.P.C.K., London, 1965, p 15

If Brooks emphasised the importance of the personality of the preacher it was as a salutary counter to that view of preaching which ascribed to the preacher the same kind of mechanical, almost automatic, inspiration which the holders of the theory of verbal inspiration ascribed to the Bible. It is not to be denied that a man's personality may come between his people and the message of God. It is true that because it is written of Jesus that 'the common people heard him gladly' it cannot therefore be assumed that every popular preacher is faithfully proclaiming the Word of God. He may be being 'heard gladly' because he is saying what people want to hear, is pandering to their prejudices, conspiring with them in their desire to escape from the demands of the Gospel. This is a real danger! But the alternative is not to seek refuge in some kind of faceless anonymity, or to pretend that we can so empty ourselves of our selves that we become like mediums out of which a voice, which is not our own, proclaims a message which we have not ourselves understood. This is psychologically impossible. It is, also, extremely dangerous for any man to pretend to others, and to himself, that he has become nothing more than a passive vehicle for the divine revelation. Even the man whose sermon consists of little more than a series of scriptural quotations, each prefaced by 'The Bible says' must not foolishly imagine that, somehow, he has successfully eliminated the human factor, effaced himself completely. It is he who has selected, and carefully selected, what the Bible says! To over-emphasise the importance of the human factor in preaching may be dangerous; but to under-emphasise it is fatal! The preacher's person, his character, personality, emotional drives, prejudices and often hidden preconceptions, are important elements in shaping his preaching. If he would preach to others he had better know himself.

The Need for Self-Knowledge.

The preacher should be aware of himself, of the kind of person he is, of his own motivation. I understand that before anyone can practise as a psycho-analyst he must himself have undergone an analysis. I would deduce that one major reason for this is that he might otherwise, unwittingly, transfer some of his own psychological problems to his patients. A preacher need not undergo an analysis as part of his preparation, but he is under an obligation constantly to examine himself. It is all too easy for a man to use the pulpit as the means whereby he expresses his own aggression or frustration. What passes for righteous indignation may be nothing more than sheer bad temper! Even when the object, or the cause, against which his indignation is directed deserves to be so treated, he still has to be sure that this is the real cause of his anger, and not merely being used as an opportunity to vent his spleen upon something. Oh the satisfaction of a glorious burst of bad temper in a righteous cause!

Much of the scolding of congregations, not perhaps so frequently indulged in as in former days, may have its origin in the preacher's hurt pride, his offended ego. Men may castigate their people for not coming to church to worship God when, in fact, they are expressing resentment that the people are not coming to church to listen to them. Many a preacher has gained a reputation for prophetic fury, whose anger was really an anger against himself, or against life; but it masqueraded in his preaching as the wrath of God against his world. Looking back through the ages one is aware of how

73

much hate, malice and all uncharitableness have at times been projected from the pulpit by men, who perhaps did not know that they were expressing themselves under the guise of speaking for God.

Allied to this is the danger that the preacher, because he is a man of his time and sensitive to the pressures of the society in which he lives, may become a kind of mouthpiece through which the anger and frustration of his congregation are expressed. This is not a role to which any man is likely, deliberately, to lend himself; but it is something against which he must be deliberately upon his guard. It is a peril of which he must be aware. There are sermons in which the preacher, though he is not aware of it, is really saying to the congregation, 'Come now and let us be angry together concerning these wicked people in that wicked world outside.'

All of us, without exception, have some deep-rooted, emotional, sometimes irrational, sometimes destructive, drives and urges of which we may not be aware. The very nature of the preacher's profession, the conventions which it imposes upon him, the patterns of behaviour expected from him, may inhibit the expression of these more than is the case for other men. They are not, however, thereby eliminated and he must beware that they do not find an outlet for their expression through his preaching, and even be sanctified in the process! The perils here are obvious. To be aware of them is essential. The only way of guarding against them is through self-knowledge: the self-knowledge which comes as one is open to God in prayer and also as one is open to one's fellow men through whom God may often speak to us. The prayer of the preacher must often be:

THE PREACHER'S PERSONALITY

'Search me, O God, and know my heart: try me, and know
my thoughts: and see if there be any wicked way in me,
and lead me in the way everlasting.'

At best, we are damaged instruments, but we must
take comfort that God can use damaged instruments. He
has had plenty of practice in this and even our weakness
may, by his grace, be used to redound to his glory, and
to the healing of his children.

The Need for Integrity.

The temptation to dishonesty is one to which the
preacher is often very vulnerable. He has to command
attention which is not always easy, but he must be
careful not to resort to cheap and shoddy stratagems in
this endeavour.

I recall a man relating to me how, on one occasion,
he attended a service in his home church when a
well-known figure in the Scottish pulpit was the visiting
preacher. He was much impressed by the manner in
which this notable divine began his sermon. He had a
sheaf of notes in his hand and said: 'My friends, this is
the sermon which I intended to preach this evening but
on my way to the church something happened which
changed my mind, and so....' and at this point he very
dramatically tore up the sheaf of notes and then
proceeded to preach, apparently extemporaneously, a
magnificent sermon. My informant was most impressed.
Some months later he was in another part of the
country and discovered that the same preacher was
conducting the service in a neighbouring church. He
decided to go and, to his profound horror, was spectator
to the same dramatic tearing up of notes, and heard the
same sermon! I knew the preacher, and found it very
difficult to reconcile this behaviour with my knowledge
of him. He was a man for whom I had a considerable

respect and I cannot understand how he could have justified such a cheap trick. It was the kind of thing which he would never have done in his ordinary every-day life. It was blatantly dishonest. No man can indulge in this kind of device without jeopardising his own spiritual life.

Similarly, it is dishonest to use as an illustration an experience which belongs to someone else and to pretend that it was your own, or to invent for yourself an experience which you have not had. There is nothing wrong in quoting another's experience, provided that you acknowledge it as not your own. Certain forms of quoting can also be subtly dishonest. In particular I abominate the quotation which is prefixed by some such phrase as, 'You will remember that Plato said...' or, 'As we all know, Karl Barth in the second volume of his *dogmatics* writes....' when the speaker knows perfectly well that his congregation will not remember 'that Plato said', and will not know 'that Barth wrote.' He is deliberately indulging in the crudest of flattery, slyly insulting the congregation by indirectly suggesting that they should know, or bent on impressing them with his own erudition. Even in what may seem such relatively small, comparatively trivial, ways the preacher must be honest; for dishonesty in the pulpit is of insidious growth and proceeds almost imperceptibly from the small to the great.

The preacher must be honest. He must be honest not only in his handling of the scriptures, to which I have already referred, but in the presentation of the message. He is not permitted to sacrifice his own integrity in order to command the attention, or the acceptance, of a congregation, important though it is that he should command their attention, and eager though he may be that they should accept his message.

76

Concerning 'borrowing', a practice which is almost universally condemned by lecturers in homiletics, I must confess that I see nothing desperately wrong with it. It is very rare for any man to have a truly original idea — and when he does, in ninety per cent. of cases, it is likely to be wrong. I know that I am debtor to all manner of people who, at different times and in different ways, have set my mind alight. If I do not read many sermons it is because I find it so difficult to forget the good ones — at any rate the ones which seem to me to be good — and they keep intruding upon me when I am studying the particular passage, or text of scripture, from which they were preached. There can be no objection to borrowing, provided of course, and the proviso is unconditional, that men acknowledge their source, and do not make borrowing a substitute for preparation; and provided, also, that what they borrow expresses exactly what they feel compelled to say. A well-known figure in the Church of Scotland used to say, 'There is no copyright in the kingdom of God.' It is a good thing he felt that way because so many people borrowed from him! He did not mean by this that there could be any excuse for plagiarism. I have an American friend who makes a point, every now and again, of preaching what he considers to be one of the great sermons. It may be a contemporary sermon, one of Niebuhr's or Martin Luther King's, or it may be one of the great sermons of the past. He tells his people what he is doing and makes no attempt to pass it off as his own. I cannot see any reason to condemn such a practice, though personally I have never made it my own. There are two principal reasons for this. I would find it difficult to identify completely with this other man's sermon, and I find the preparation of sermons such hard work that I might, once I started, be too readily tempted to adopt this as an easy way out.

The demand for integrity on the part of the preacher goes deeper than anything I have, as yet, mentioned. It involves, for example, the place of emotion in preaching. Clearly emotion is an important element in life, a part of a man's total experience, and if we are to appeal to the whole man his emotions cannot be ignored. One must appeal to the heart as well as to the reason, the conscience and the will. It is, however, of fundamental importance that the appeal be honest. No preacher has the right deliberately to play upon the emotions of a congregation, to pretend to an emotion which he himself does not feel, in order to create an emotional response from others. There are circumstances in which it may be all too easy to do this, but it must not be done. The attempt deliberately to manipulate people is a gross misuse of the pulpit, and no man of any integrity will ever resort to it.

People will often impute to a minister a kind of goodness which he does not possess, and which he does not want to possess, because he does not accept that this professional goodness attributed to him is real goodness at all. It is merely a conventional behaviour pattern associated with the clergy. The pressure to conform to it can, however, be very strong and he may be tempted into becoming a man with a double standard, and seek to justify his professional front because, he argues, if it were discarded, the weaker brethren might be offended. The ministerial voice, the ministerial manner, both fortunately less common now, are part of this charade: perhaps only the more obvious parts. A man may think that this is how a minister is expected to speak, this is what a minister is expected to say, this is how a minister is expected to act; and be persuaded to adopt the role which other people have cast for him. The consequence is an artificial person, a person who does not ring true. No less artificial, is the 'with it' parson who is so determined to be a 'man among men' that he takes his colour, like the chameleon, from his surroundings and, rightly, forfeits all respect thereby.

Some years ago I heard the Rev. Vernon Proxton of the Religious Broadcasting Department of the B.B.C. speak at a meeting of the General Assembly of the Presbyterian Church of England. He told a parable from Kierkegaard which has remained with me to haunt and disturb me.

> A circus proprietor discovered that the big tent was on fire, and he called one of his employees and said, 'Go into the middle of the circus ring and tell the people that the tent is on fire and they must get out as quickly as they can.' The man went, but in a little while he came back saying, 'They would not listen to me! They only laughed at me!' 'Go again', said the proprietor, 'and make them listen! Say to them the circus is on fire, flee for your lives!' But again he returned, saying, 'They laughed at me! They refused to listen to me!' Because the man whom the circus proprietor had sent was the clown; and no one took the clown seriously.

The stage clergyman is unquestionably a figure of fun, a grotesque caricature. Yet, if we are honest, we have to confess that there is an element of truth in the distortion. We would not otherwise find it funny. We would not otherwise recognise that it is a caricature. We have, therefore, to go further and confess that, in some measure, we, the preachers, are ourselves responsible for this caricature, that if people see us this way, there must be some reason for them seeing us this way. The reason has, I would maintain, something to do with the mask which the minister can all too easily assume. Here again the need is for personal integrity. This is not a plea that we should seek self-consciously to change the 'image' — magic word! — of the minister, rather it is a plea that we should altogether forget about images.

The Need for Courage.

If the preacher is faithful to the scriptures he must, again and again, challenge the cultural pretensions of the age in which he lives, the prejudices, the preconceptions, of the people to whom he speaks in the name of God. This will require courage. The more you come to know and to love the people to whom you speak the more courage you will require, since the more you may be tempted to blunt the cutting edge of the Gospel for fear of hurting them, or forfeiting their esteem.

It is easy for a man to acquire a spurious reputation for boldness by attacking the vices which all his people would agree to be vices, and from which most of them would be able honestly to claim that they are free. It is easy for a man to acquire a spurious reputation for boldness by indulging in a kind of irresponsible moralism which calls for sacrifices to be made by others, which he well knows he himself will never be called upon to make; or which presents as simple, clear cut issues of good and evil, problems which all who are involved in them know to be far more subtle and complex than he allows. This is not courage. This is presumption! But to preach the Word of God today, over and against the assumptions of a highly materialistic and affluent society, against the background of nuclear warfare and the blasphemy of racialism, in the situations in which these are live issues and not academic ones; this requires courage. It may sometimes mean that you are accused of meddling in politics, but I find it hard to believe that anyone can read the Old Testament and the New Testament and seriously maintain that the preacher should, or can, abstain from all comment on politics. Even more, perhaps, it takes courage to be open to men and women and not to hide behind some pseudo clerical authority.

The Need for Compassion.

It is impossible to separate preaching from one's pastoral relationships with people. Only as the preacher is a man who knows the language, the thought and the experiences of other men and women will he be able to express the eternal truth of the Gospel in terms which are meaningful for their lives in this world. Unless he has sat where they sit, and understands something of the lives they live, and has listened to them speak about the kind of lives they live, he will be unable to communicate with them. He must have heard them speak about the lives they live. This is important.

On one occasion, shortly after my coming to a new congregation, I had visited one of the districts with the district elder and he said to me at the close of our visitation. 'I've been an elder of this district for fifteen years and I know more about these people now than I ever did before. You see I never liked to ask them outright what they did, in case they thought I was prying, but you asked every one of them about their work tonight.' It is important to know something about the work of the people to whom you are to minister. How else can you make the necessary effort to enter imaginatively into their situation? If you are going to pray for them as you ought, you should know how they spend the greater part of their days.

Above all, unless he loves, the preacher will not be able to communicate with people. If he loves they will know it, and listen even when he has hard things to say. Whenever a man or woman in some kind of distress says of his or her minister, 'I don't feel I could speak to him', or, 'He would not understand,' or, 'I am ashamed to tell the minister,' there has been a tragic breakdown in communication. Somehow, somewhere in his preaching the minister has given the impression of a harsh moral rectitude, or a lack of compassion, which has made him appear unapproachable. It need hardly be added that the confidence of people given in a pastoral relationship is sacred, and must never be broken.

The Need for Humility.

The pulpit is a dangerous place because it is a place of authority.

The preacher can pontificate on any subject without interruption, and even imagine that, because no one interrupts, everyone is agreeing with, and accepting, what he has to say. It is sometimes difficult for a man to avoid taking to himself the authority of the message which he has been commanded to deliver. Not that one does this consciously. But I have noticed in myself, on occasion, an instinctive hostility to criticism, a reaction which I believe is not uncommon even among theologians!

We talk much in these days about the place of the laymen in the Church, but I sometimes wonder how much attention we do, in fact, give to them. The tendency to speak of the church as 'my church' and to think of myself as someone who is in charge of it is perhaps symptomatic. I was pulled up, very gently and courteously, by one of my elders at a recent Kirk Session Conference at which men spoke more freely

THE PREACHER'S PERSONALITY

than they are wont to do at Session Meetings. He said, "You often say at a Kirk Session Meeting 'it has been decided' and I find myself asking 'but who decided it?' "

The preacher is the expert, the professional, and there is a real danger that he may be found lacking in what is an essential requirement, a proper humility. In this connection the story of the washing of the disciples' feet is one which should never be far from our thoughts. We should note that there was not one of the disciples who would have been unwilling to wash Christ's feet; no question about that! What stuck in the throat of each and every one of them, and none could swallow, was that he should wash the feet of those others who, in his heart of hearts, he regarded as inferior; or, at any rate, no better than himself. There was not one of them who would not gladly have washed Christ's feet, but that was not the point. The point was that they should be willing to wash one another's feet. The point was not that they should be willing to be Christ's servants, it was the much more difficult one that they should be willing to be the servants of others!

A man can call himself a 'servant of the Lord' and still be as proud as Lucifer among men. Indeed he can be proud of his position as a servant of the Lord and use it to exercise authority over others. This was what these men wanted. Not one of them wanted to take precedence over Christ, but each wanted to take precedence over his fellows. What Jesus said was not, 'If I have washed your feet, you ought, also, to wash my feet,' but, 'You ought, also, to wash one another's feet.' Your authority is the authority of a servant, a servant of the Word and a servant of the congregation.

The Need to Accept Fellowship.
The man in the pulpit is in the very nature of

things isolated, not only when he is in the pulpit but throughout the rest of his life. It is interesting to note that in those churches which still have seat rents the more expensive seats are, often, those which are furthest away from the minister. He is in a position different from that of any of his brethren in the congregation. He has a task which they do not have and, in consequence, he must accept a measure of loneliness and isolation. It has sometimes seemed to me that the preacher himself may intensify this isolation by deliberately choosing to keep himself apart. He is not under the discipline of the Kirk Session — this is probably wise — instead he is under the discipline of the Presbytery and in effect, especially in the larger Presbyteries, this has become a court which is much more concerned with getting through its business than with discipline and fellowship. The consequence is that the preacher may well find himself denied the discipline and support of a Christian fellowship. Yet he needs it as much as, perhaps more than, any of his brethren in the Kirk Session or the congregation. He may look for it among his personal friends in the ministry, but this is not where he should find it. He should find it in the congregation to which he ministers and which, in a very real sense, must minister to him, and often would if only he would allow it. But somewhere he has been told that 'familiarity breeds contempt' and does not realise that familiarity only breeds contempt for those who earn contempt. The minister must not be afraid of the fellowship he preaches; and sometimes I think he is.

The Need for Self Discipline.

Most men, in other occupations, have an external discipline imposed upon them by the conditions of their work. They have to be at the office, the shop, the

84

factory or on duty between certain strictly prescribed hours though of course many, particularly in the professions, doctors, lawyers, teachers, work far beyond the minimum hours demanded of them. The minister does not have this external discipline to anything like the same extent. No man can be as lazy as a minister can, if he wants. No man can be so busy, in the wrong sense, in a kind of phrenetic activity, as the minister. He must discipline himself in the use of his time, and this is not always easy. Nor is the difficulty lessened by the multiplicity of the demands which can be made upon his time. There are always innumerable things he could be doing, but there are only twelve hours in a day and his capacity for work is no greater than that of other men.

The principal peril is that he does not allow sufficient time for the task of preparation for preaching. It does require hard study and hard thinking, and the chief enemy is not the demands which our people make upon us but the sloth which makes us escape into other forms of activity, good in themselves but, in this instance, the enemies of the best. A man should endeavour to keep office hours in his study. He should set aside certain times for study, and should strive to observe them as rigorously as if he had a boss or foreman standing over him. He should be able to say, 'I start work at nine in the morning,' and be in his study at nine and from then until one, or whatever be the hour upon which he has decided. Of course this is not always possible, and there are inevitable and necessary interruptions of one's schedule, but this is what his aim should be.

This may seem very elementary but it needs to be said, and kept constantly in mind. Make sure that you have the time to study, to read, and keep reading the kind of stuff which will stretch your mind. Keep in touch with theology. Keep in touch with modern thought. Read modern literature. You may not always like what you read but it will help you to feel the pulse of the world in which you have to preach. One lesser, but not unimportant, benefit to be derived from reading is the constant familiarity with words which are the tools of your trade. I am sure that it is profitable to keep a commonplace book in which you take notes of your reading. I wish that I could do this, but I read very quickly and dislike having to stop and take notes and, therefore, I rely, perhaps too much, on my ability to remember where I read something and how to find it. Make sure that you have time to read and study.

Perhaps the most difficult and yet the most necessary discipline of all is the discipline of prayer. This is where we are most likely to fall short. Yet it is here that we see ourselves as we are before God, here that we are made aware of our subtle temptations to dishonesty, our failures in integrity. It is in prayer that we find the courage we require, and here that we remember those people to whom we must speak. It is here that our compassion and our understanding are both widened and deepened. This is the place to learn humility and to be cleansed of pride and vanity. This is where we receive. Unless we receive we have nothing to give. It is not enough to have worked long over a sermon if we have not prayed over it. It seems so simple and so obvious and yet it is so hard to be faithful, and all our worst failures begin with our failure here. It has been said that to work is to pray. I often wish that I could accept that it is as simple as that, but I know that one can work, and work very hard, without praying and can be so busy doing God's work that we do not pause to ask if what we are doing is really what he wants done.

To pray is, also, to work; and, conscious of my own failures, I would say that, for many of us, it is the hardest work of all.

The Need for Enthusiasm.

Finally, the man who preaches must have a genuine enthusiasm, a true zeal for his task. If he lacks this, if preaching has become just another tiresome duty, reluctantly undertaken; if he no longer has any conviction about the importance of the proclamation of the Gospel through preaching: then let him find something else to do. Perhaps we should recognise that this sometimes does happen. It need not mean that the individual concerned has lost his faith; only that he has lost his desire to serve the Gospel in this way. It need not mean that he will serve it any the less effectively in some other way. He should not feel that, somehow, it is incumbent upon him to go on going through the motions when the desire, the compulsion are no longer present. Perhaps as a Church we should be considering whether, for some men, the Ministry of the Word may be something to which they do not necessarily devote their whole lives. We gladly accept men as being called to the ministry who have been ten, twenty, even thirty years in some other employment; but we still tend to feel that if a man leaves the ministry after ten years this represents failure, loss of faith.

The preacher must want to preach, even if, at the same time, he is burdened and frightened by the thought of it. He must want to preach, more than he wants to do anything else. This is what I mean by enthusiasm, and the word is not inappropriate if you remember the derivation of it.

Christ did not say, 'Follow me and you will become fishers of men.' He said, 'Follow me and I will make you fishers of men.' The fulfilment of this promise came at Pentecost with the outpouring of the Holy Spirit. It was then that the disciples were made fishers of men. If we accept Christ's invitation to follow him, and if we seek to obey him, then we are not left to our own devices and our own strength; then comes the power which enables us to do what is demanded of us; then we are made fishers of men. Without this we can do nothing. Without this, however orthodox our doctrine, it is dead and lifeless. Without this, however complete our knowledge of the Bible, it is of no avail. Without this, however impeccable our Church Order, it is but dry bones.

When Paul met the followers of Apollos he asked them only one question, 'Received ye the Holy Spirit when ye believed?' Not: 'What were you taught?' Not: 'Who laid hands upon you to confirm you?' But, 'Did you receive the Holy Spirit?' It is this 'enthusiasm', and this alone, which can enable us truly to be followers of Christ and fishers of men. But this is promised to those who are willing to surrender their lives in obedience to Christ and to accept his invitation: 'Follow me and I will make you fishers of men.'

I sometimes hear kindly people expressing their sympathy for young men entering the ministry of the Church today. Few would deny that there are special difficulties and problems peculiar to the age in which we live, but I do not feel sorry for those who are entering the ministry today. I would consider that it was insulting to be sorry for them. It is a tremendous task, an impossible task, but made possible by the grace of God. It is, for those who feel 'called to preach', the most exhilarating, exciting and satisfying task they could ever wish to be given. I am not sorry for them. I am happy for them.

THE PREACHER'S PERSONALITY

Let me conclude with the prayer of an old Russian liturgy quoted by Phillips Brooks as 'The Preacher's Prayer'.

'O Lord and Sovereign of my life take from me the spirit of idleness, despair, love of power and unprofitable speaking.'